La Salle and his men continued their journey down the Mississippi in canoes

STORIES OF AMERICAN EXPLORERS AND SETTLERS

BY

SARAH DOW HEARD
AND
M. W. KING

ILLUSTRATED BY
EDWIN J. PRITTIE

THE JOHN C. WINSTON COMPANY
CHICAGO PHILADELPHIA TORONTO
ATLANTA SAN FRANCISCO DALLAS

Copyright, 1933, by
THE JOHN C. WINSTON COMPANY

Copyright in Great Britain
The British Dominions and Possessions
Copyright in the Philippine Islands

All rights reserved

PRINTED IN THE U.S.A.
AT THE INTERNATIONAL PRESS
THE JOHN C. WINSTON COMPANY, PROPRIETORS,
PHILADELPHIA

FOREWORD

GEOGRAPHY AND HISTORY

The soft glow of the reading light fell on the yellow pages of an old book from which a mother had been reading to her boys. It was her grandfather's diary. Both boys were bending over the back of her chair to see the faded, old-fashioned writing. How thrilling the story had been, full of courage, hard work, and brave adventure. And best of all, it was a true story. As she closed the book, the mother said, "That is the history of the first man to build a house in this part of our state."

The older boy was already studying history in school, but the younger one did not know the meaning of the word *history*. "Mother," he said, "do you call it 'history' because it is 'his story'?"

The question was a good one because the diary was history and it was also Grandfather's story. The mother explained that our word *history* is not made by joining together two smaller words, but it comes to us from the early Greeks, who used the word *historia* which is nearly the same as our own word *history*. History is a complete story of real men, women, and children. The history of each man differs from that of any other person. There are two reasons for this: people themselves differ from one another; their surroundings as they live and work are different.

When a boy, this pioneer grandfather had been one of three brothers who lived on a rocky hillside near the Atlantic coast. Their father earned his living by fishing. As soon as one of the boys was old enough, he helped his father manage the boat and bring in the fish. If this boy had lived near the iron mines of western Pennsylvania, he might have become a miner instead of a fisherman. Another brother loved adventure. If he had lived near a forest, he might have been a hunter and fur trader; but because he often saw ships sailing to far-off lands, he became a sailor. In time, he grew to be a sea captain with a ship of his own.

The pioneer grandfather liked to work in the fields. He could have stayed at home and plowed and planted the rough, stony land. In exchange for very hard work, his crops might have given him enough food, clothing, and shelter. But this boy knew that land better suited for farming could be found in the West, and he had courage enough to make the journey. He became not only a prosperous farmer but also a leading citizen in that new western country.

The history of each of these boys was largely influenced by the place where he lived and by the things that he found with which to work. The fish, the open sea, and the fertile plains were gifts which nature had placed in different parts of the world. Each of the boys had to learn to use the special gift which he found in the place where he chose to live. He had to learn the lesson well if he expected to be comfortable and happy. If, instead of farming, the pioneer grandfather had tried to dig for gold, he soon would have starved.

The history of a nation is also influenced by the kind of land on which its people live. If you wish to understand the history of this country, you must learn all that you can about the geography of the United States. When you need information about the mountains, rivers, climate, and products of some part of the world, you study geography.

But history is not an independent study. History needs geography to help make it clear and interesting. As you read these *Stories of American Explorers and Settlers*, you will find that part of each story is really geography. You will also learn that the great men of history were those who learned nature's lessons. They were the men who taught others to use the gifts which nature has so generously given to the world.

CONTENTS

	PAGE
FOREWORD — GEOGRAPHY AND HISTORY	iii

THE DISCOVERY OF AMERICA — CHRISTOPHER COLUMBUS 1

Boyhood Days of Columbus	4
The Plan of Sailing Around the World	6
He Seeks Help from Spain	6
Preparations for the Journey	8
Sailing Westward	9
Land	13
Still Searching for the East	15
Finding the Important Points	18
Using a Map	18

AROUND THE WORLD — FERDINAND MAGELLAN. 20

Exploring the New World	20
Ferdinand Magellan	21
The Voyage	24
On the Pacific Ocean	29
Proof That the Earth Is Round	32
The One Important Thought	32

THE DISCOVERY OF FLORIDA — PONCE DE LEON 34

The Gifts of the New World	34
Juan Ponce de Leon	36
Ponce de Leon Tries to Settle in Florida	43
How Well Do You Remember?	44

SPAIN CONQUERS MEXICO — HERNANDO CORTÉS 45

The Desire for Gold	45
Cortés in Mexico City	50
Cortés Ordered to Cuba	53
The Aztec Attack	54
Cortés Conquers the Aztecs	58
Study Helps	59

CONTENTS

SPANIARDS IN THE SOUTHWEST — DE SOTO, CORONADO, MISSIONARIES.................. 60

- Gold Makes Spain Wealthy............................. 60
- Ferdinand De Soto.................................... 61
- Discovery of the Mississippi.......................... 63
- Coronado Searches for the Seven Cities................ 64
- Missionaries in the Southwest......................... 67
- Father Junipero Serra................................. 69
- Spanish America....................................... 71
- Making and Answering Questions........................ 72
- Something to Think About.............................. 72

THE SPANISH ARMADA — SIR FRANCIS DRAKE.. 73

- The Boyhood of Francis Drake.......................... 73
- Drake Clashes with the Spaniards...................... 74
- The Master Thief of the Western World................. 75
- Drake Sails on the Pacific Ocean...................... 78
- Sailing West to Reach England......................... 81
- Drake and the Spanish Armada.......................... 83
- Reading and Remembering............................... 87

ENGLISH IN THE NEW WORLD — JOHN CABOT, WALTER RALEIGH........................ 88

- John Cabot.. 88
- Walter Raleigh.. 90
- Walter Raleigh's Colonies............................. 92
- Making an Outline..................................... 97
- Something to Think About.............................. 97

THE JAMESTOWN COLONY — CAPTAIN JOHN SMITH.. 98

- Early Adventures...................................... 98
- The First Permanent English Settlement in America..... 98
- Adventures with the Indians........................... 102
- More Lazy Gold Hunters................................ 105
- Smith Rules the Colony................................ 107
- Filling in an Outline................................. 111

THE PILGRIMS IN PLYMOUTH — MILES STANDISH.................................... 112

- The Puritans and the Pilgrims......................... 112
- Sailing to the New World.............................. 115
- Choosing a Location for the New Colony................ 116
- Building Homes in Plymouth............................ 119
- Help from the Indians................................. 120
- The First Thanksgiving................................ 123
- Filling in an Outline................................. 125

CONTENTS

ix

PAGE

PROVIDENCE, RHODE ISLAND — Roger Williams... 127
Williams Disagrees with Puritan Beliefs...................... 127
Williams Is Forced to Flee................................. 129
The Providence Colony Started............................. 131
Roger Williams Saves His Enemies.......................... 133
Acting the Story.. 136
Things to Think About.................................... 136

THE QUAKERS IN PENNSYLVANIA — William Penn... 137
William Penn Becomes a Quaker............................ 137
A Quaker Colony in America............................... 142
Penn Comes to America................................... 145
Asking and Answering Questions........................... 148

THE NORTHWEST PASSAGE — Henry Hudson.. 149
Seeking New Routes....................................... 149
Henry Hudson.. 150
The Journey of the *Half Moon*............................ 152
Hudson Sails to America................................... 153
The Last Voyage.. 157
How Carefully Did You Read?.............................. 160

THE SETTLEMENT OF NEW YORK — Peter Stuyvesant.. 161
The Dutch Settle on Manhattan Island...................... 161
Stuyvesant Becomes Governor.............................. 162
Dutch and English Claims to New Netherland............... 165
Making a Summary.. 168

THE FRENCH IN CANADA — Samuel de Champlain.. 170
Early Life in France....................................... 170
Champlain Learns about America........................... 170
Champlain Plants a Colony at Quebec...................... 173
Champlain and the Indians................................ 174
Champlain's Life in Canada................................ 177
Completing an Outline.................................... 179

DOWN THE MISSISSIPPI — Robert La Salle... 181
Searching for the Mississippi River......................... 181
Robert La Salle... 183
La Salle Meets Many Difficulties........................... 186
Down the Mississippi..................................... 192
Lost but Not Discouraged................................. 195
Finding Your Way... 196

CONTENTS

PAGE

THE FRENCH AND INDIAN WAR — WOLFE AND MONTCALM 197

Rival Claims in the New World............................. 197
The Struggle for the Ohio River Valley.................... 198
William Pitt and Victory.................................. 202
Wolfe and Montcalm.. 203
Making an Outline... 206

ENGLAND AND HER COLONIES — AMERICAN PATRIOTS 208

Progress in the Thirteen English Colonies................. 208
Benjamin Franklin... 210
Duty of American Colonies toward England.................. 213
The Quarrel Begins.. 215
The Orator of the Revolution.............................. 218
The Colonists Resist the Stamp Act........................ 219
Growing Trouble in the Colonies........................... 221
Drifting toward War....................................... 225
Reporting on a Topic...................................... 230

THE REVOLUTIONARY WAR — GEORGE WASHINGTON 231

Early Training of George Washington....................... 231
Early Services for His Country............................ 233
Washington Becomes Commander in Chief..................... 236
The Declaration of Independence........................... 238
Hard Times for the Colonies............................... 239
Fighting for Freedom...................................... 242
Franklin Seeks Help from France........................... 246
Fighting in the South..................................... 248
The Surrender at Yorktown................................. 249
Peace... 252
From United Colonies to United States..................... 254
Reporting on a Topic...................................... 256

INDEX 259

THE DISCOVERY OF AMERICA

CHRISTOPHER COLUMBUS

Boyhood Days of Columbus

The hot sun of Italy beat down on the green water in the harbor at Genoa. Its scorching rays pelted the crowd of men and boys standing on the dock. But the people did not mind the sun. They were watching a big ship that had just returned from a long trip. Most of its orange sails were furled, but all its flags were flying as it moved slowly to the wharf.

"Here it comes," shouted one of the boys, who almost fell into the water in his excitement. With a swish of the waves, the big boat slid up to the dock and the sailors tied her fast. Soon men began to unload the ship's cargo, which was made up of bales of rugs and fine silk cloth, and boxes of pepper, cloves, and other spices.

Not many of the boys at the wharf could stay to watch the unloading, certainly not Christopher and Bartolomeo Columbus, the two sons of the wool weaver. They had to go home to help their father wash the wool that was stacked in his shop. After the wool had been washed, their father would comb and weave it into cloth. As the two boys walked home, they talked of the ship.

"Some day I am going to sail away on a ship like that," said Christopher.

"We'll both be sailors," said Bartolomeo.

Genoa was a large city. Many ships from many countries came into its harbor. Christopher and his brother liked to watch the ships. Whenever they could, the two boys went down to the wharves to play. Sometimes they saw the cargoes being loaded and unloaded. Often they listened to the talk of the sailors who liked to boast about their adventures.

Italian merchants sent their ships eastward across the Mediterranean Sea to land at the ports of western Asia and buy the rare products of India, China, and the East Indies. This route was full of danger. There were pirates who watched for a chance to attack merchant ships and steal their rich cargoes. There were also bold seamen from other countries who wanted to gain this trade with the East for their own merchants.

The boys heard many a story of sea fights and adventures with Turkish pirates on the Mediterranean Sea. They also heard of strange, far-away western oceans. Sometimes a sailor would answer their eager questions.

"Yes," he would say, "I've been to the torrid sea. I went on a Portuguese boat."

"Was the weather hot there," the boys would ask, "and did the water boil?"

"Yes, the weather was very hot, but the water did not boil. There is nothing to that old story. I never did believe it; and the other one about the falling-off place is just as foolish."

"But you did not go far out of sight of land, did you?"

"No, we followed the African coast southward. But I was not afraid," he would boast. "I shall go again as soon as I get a chance."

As the boys grew older, they often talked about the sea and the trips they hoped to make some day. Were there really monsters in the great Sea of Darkness west of Europe? And did ships really fall over the edge of the world if they went too far west? "Some day I'm going to find out," said Christopher.

As soon as he was old enough, Christopher Columbus learned to be a sailor. He went on many voyages. At one time, as he was sailing along the shore of Portugal, a pirate ship attacked the boat he was on and sank it. But Columbus swam ashore, and after that lived in Portugal.

Portugal was the country for a bold sailor like Columbus. Prince Henry, whose father was the king, wanted to find a new water route to India. Portugal could then gain some of the profitable trade which was bringing wealth to Italian cities. Prince Henry believed that the East Indies could be reached by sailing around the southern end of Africa and turning east. Each year he sent the best sailors he could find on exploring trips.

On your map the route around Africa is very easy to find. But the maps which these sailors used showed only the northern part of Africa. No one knew how big it was, nor how far south the land extended. Every year Prince Henry's ships sailed a little farther south along the African coast. But when Columbus came to Portugal, no one had yet found the way around Africa.

Columbus lived in Portugal for several years. Between voyages he learned how to draw maps and how to use instruments for guiding a ship on its course. He read the books of travelers, such as Marco Polo, who had once visited the ruler of China. He also studied all the books he could find about the earth and the stars. The more Columbus studied, the more he agreed with the wise scholars who claimed that the earth is round.

The Plan of Sailing Around the World

Then a great idea came to him. If the world is round, why not sail westward to reach the rich countries of the East? Neither Turks nor Italians could interfere with such a route.

The plan was simple, but it was not easy to carry out. Columbus did not have enough money to buy the ships and hire the sailors that he would need for the voyage. Besides, it would not be easy to find men brave enough to go on such a trip.

CHRISTOPHER COLUMBUS

Nearly all the sailors still believed that great monsters lived in the Atlantic Ocean. They still called the Atlantic Ocean the Sea of Darkness.

Columbus talked to some of his friends about his idea. They did not listen to him. "He is just a dreamer," they thought. "No man would really sail on such a dangerous voyage."

Then Columbus wrote to a great scholar in Italy and asked his advice. This great man, Toscanelli, answered the letter, encouraging Columbus. Both he and Columbus made a great mistake, however. They thought that the earth was much smaller than it really is. Of course they did not dream that the great continent of America was between Europe and China.

Columbus drew maps showing India, China, and the East Indies as he expected to find them on the other side of the Sea of Darkness. Then he marked the course which he wished to sail, and showed by his charts that the way would be shorter and easier than the route which the Portuguese sailors were still trying to find around Africa.

Columbus took these papers to the king of Portugal and explained his plans. He asked the king to supply ships for the great adventure.

The king asked his wise men what they thought of the plan. They laughed and said that Columbus was crazy. "Everyone with common sense knows that the world is flat," they said. "If it were round, the people who live on the other side would have to walk as if they were on a ceiling with their heads hanging down. The water in the lakes and rivers might drop off the earth. Columbus is just a foolish dreamer."

The king of Portugal did not help to carry out the great plan. Then Columbus took his little boy Diego, and left Portugal to find help somewhere else.

He Seeks Help from Spain

Some time passed, and one day a dusty traveler and a young boy walked into the town of Palos, a small seaport of Spain. It was Christopher Columbus and his son. On a hill back of the town stood the convent of La Rabida. The kind monks were sure to welcome all who came; so the two travelers climbed the hill. At the gate of the convent they knocked and asked for water. As they stood talking to the gatekeeper, Friar Juan Perez saw them and asked them to come in and rest. Columbus gladly accepted the invitation.

That evening as they enjoyed the cool breeze from the ocean, Columbus talked to the friendly monk about his desire to sail westward to find the East. Friar Perez was much interested in this idea and asked two friends to come and listen to the plan. These men looked at the maps which Columbus carried and listened to his explanations. They were convinced that such a voyage as Columbus planned would be successful. They even

CHRISTOPHER COLUMBUS

offered to go with him whenever he was ready to start.

The next morning Columbus left little Diego with the monks and set out to ask the aid of the king and queen of Spain. A war was going on at this time with the Moors, people from northern Africa who had conquered a part of Spain. King Ferdinand and Queen Isabella listened to Columbus, but they were much more interested in driving the Moors out of Spain than they were in finding a new route to India. Columbus saw that he would have to wait until the war was ended before he could get help from Spain.

He drew maps and did whatever he could to support himself while he waited for his chance. Days, weeks, even years went by, while he waited and worked. He grew poorer all the time and his hair grew whiter, but he would not give up. Finally the Spanish army conquered the Moors, and the king and queen had time to think of other things. Columbus decided to go to them again and ask for help to carry out his great plan.

His friend, Friar Perez, wrote from the convent to the queen and urged her to listen to Columbus. Then Queen Isabella sent for Columbus. He came and told her all about his thrilling plan. This time the queen was very much interested in the idea of sailing west to trade with the East Indies. She thought that Columbus was a daring seaman who might bring riches and honor to Spain. She decided that he must be given a chance to carry out his plan.

King Ferdinand was afraid that Spain had not enough money left from the war to buy ships for Columbus. "I will sell my own jewels if there is no other way to get money," said Queen Isabella.

At first Columbus could hardly believe the good news. He was made an admiral of Spain and was promised the honor of becoming governor of all the lands which he should discover and claim for King Ferdinand and Queen Isabella. His son, Diego, who was now a big boy, was made a page at the royal court.

Preparations for the Journey

Columbus went at once to Palos to prepare for the voyage. There was much to be done. Ships must be chosen and supplied with food, water, and everything needed to last for many months. Most important of all, men who were willing to go on so long and dangerous a voyage had to be found.

Three small vessels were made ready, the *Santa Maria*, the *Pinta*, and the *Niña*. They had gaily painted square sails and floated the royal Spanish banner, a green cross on a white background. The *Santa Maria* was also flying the admiral's flag. Only this flagship, which was a little larger than the others, was covered with a full deck. The *Pinta* and the *Niña* had small cabins at each end, but in the middle they were open to all the storms and winds. The ships were supplied with guns and rows of oars. These last could be used if there was a calm. Columbus and his friends felt that they had "as good ships as there were afloat."

What a difference we should see if one of these boats were floating by the side of a great ocean liner today. We could hardly believe that men were bold enough to sail out into an unknown sea in such tiny vessels. We wonder how men could live week after week in such small ships.

It was hard to persuade sailors to agree to go on this wild journey. They repeated every fearful story they had heard about the Sea of Darkness and its monsters. Fortunately for Columbus, the two friends whom he had met at the convent stood by him. One of these was a man named Pinzon, who was well-known in Palos as a brave and wise sea captain. He went from house to house encouraging the sailors and saying, "Come with us. We are going to a land where the houses have roofs of gold." The sailors forgot the sea monsters and began to talk about the great riches of that faraway land. Through the help of Pinzon, Columbus finally hired one hundred twenty men for the voyage.

Sailing Westward

At last everything was ready for the great adventure. Shining and clean and decked with flowers, the three little sailing vessels lay at anchor in the harbor of Palos. The town was at the wharf at dawn on the third day of August, 1492. The last moment had come, the last good-by had been said. As Christopher Columbus stood on the deck of the *Santa Maria*, the flags fluttered in the breeze. The moorings were loosed and the ships moved forward. The townspeople watched until the ships were no longer in sight. The daring voyage had begun.

On the third day out, the *Pinta* made a distress signal. Her rudder was broken, perhaps by two of the crew who hoped that their ship would be left behind. Columbus had no idea of giving up one of his little fleet. The ships were near the Canary Islands. Here the rudder was repaired. When they had taken on a fresh supply of wood and water, all three vessels set out again toward the west.

For three days after they left the Canary Islands, there was a calm. Not a breath of wind stirred. Finally, early on the morning of the ninth of September, a fine breeze filled the sails. The sailors watched till the last rocky coast of the Canary Islands could no longer be seen. As they turned to face the great unknown west, even the bravest heart sank.

Columbus knew how timid his men were. He knew that they believed that the Sea of Darkness held monsters which could overturn the ships and devour the sailors. Each dark night they feared that the ships might be drawn into a whirlpool

CHRISTOPHER COLUMBUS

Columbus watched eagerly for signs of land

which would pull them down under the waves. Many days after they had left the Canary Islands, the frightened sailors saw parts of a wrecked ship. Such a sight added to their terror. Columbus tried in every way to keep his men cheered and encouraged.

THE DISCOVERY OF AMERICA

He told them about the gold and the rich treasures which could be found in the countries of the East. He reminded them of the reward which the queen had offered to the man who should first sight land.

Sometimes false hopes were aroused, only to end in disappointment. One day the sea was covered with seaweeds. The plants looked so fresh and green that it seemed as if land must be near. On one of the patches of weed a live crab was floating. When the sun went down that evening, the men expected that morning light would show them land. But when morning came, there was nothing to be seen but the same tangled mass of seaweed. Then the crew was sure that the ocean was growing shallow. Perhaps they were near the falling-off place! But Columbus quieted these fears by dropping a weighted line into the water. It sank far down without reaching bottom.

Week after week passed and no land appeared. The sailors began to despair. They said, "We have already traveled farther west than any other ship. Is Columbus crazy? Are we to sail on till we die?"

But Columbus would not listen to them when they begged him to turn back, and at last some of the sailors were ready to kill their brave leader.

CHRISTOPHER COLUMBUS

The Spanish admiral was rowed ashore

Columbus knew of their plots, but he did not show the least fear. Fortunately, each time the crew was at the point of mutiny, signs of land were seen, and the men forgot everything else in their excited joy. But with each fresh disappointment, the sailors grew more and more restless and angry.

Land

After more than two months of weary waiting, sure signs of land were seen — floating pieces of wood, a branch with red berries, and many birds. Then one happy night a light appeared. The next day they saw land. That day was October 12, 1492.

The ships sailed as near as they could to the low shore and dropped their anchors. Columbus put on his finest clothes. He expected very soon to be taken before a great king living in one of the golden palaces about which Marco Polo had written. The Spanish admiral looked very grand as he stepped into a boat and was rowed ashore. He carried his sword in one hand and the flag of Spain in the other.

As soon as the sailors stepped out of the boat, they were so thankful to be on solid ground once more that they knelt down and kissed the earth. Columbus lifted the Spanish flag and claimed the new land for King Ferdinand and Queen Isabella of Spain.

Columbus had found a beautiful place. The trees, plants, and birds looked very much as he expected them to look from the books which he had read. He felt sure that he had reached one of the islands of the East Indies.

As he looked around, he saw some natives hiding among the trees and watching the newcomers. At first these men would not come near, but soon they lost their fear and came out from their hiding places. The men were reddish brown in color and wore almost no clothes. Columbus called the natives "Indians," for he was sure that he had landed on an island of the East Indies. That is how our American Indians received their name.

For many weeks the three Spanish ships sailed among the islands that we now call the West Indies. Each time that Columbus landed, he was sure that he had found the mainland of India or China and that the wonderful cities described by Marco

CHRISTOPHER COLUMBUS

Polo must be near by. At last the *Pinta* became separated from the other ships, and the *Santa Maria* was wrecked on a sandbar. Columbus had to sail back to Spain in his smallest boat, the little *Niña*.

The voyage home was a stormy one, but all ended happily. The *Pinta* was found, and the two ships sailed joyfully into the port of Palos. How the townsfolk welcomed the voyagers! Crowds of people followed Columbus, the great admiral, whenever he appeared in public. The poor man who had once walked the streets in ragged clothes was now given every honor.

The king and queen of Spain were much pleased with their brave admiral, and listened with interest as he told of all his adventures. But King Ferdinand and Queen Isabella had not forgotten that they were looking for spices and gold. Soon they sent Columbus back across the ocean to find the rich cities of the East and to start the trade which Spain wanted so much.

Still Searching for the East

On the second voyage, Columbus had no trouble getting ships and men. This time seventeen vessels and fifteen hundred men were ready to sail. Some of these people left their homes to stay in the new land which they thought was the East Indies.

When this second fleet reached the New World, the men built houses on what is now the island of

Haiti. Columbus named the settlement "Isabella" in honor of the queen. He was made governor of this first colony of white people in America.

The people of the new settlement expected soon to become rich. But when they did not find gold, silver, and fine silks, they began to complain to the Spanish king and queen about their governor. Poor Columbus did not have such a happy home-coming when he returned to Spain from this second trip. But he was still patient and persistent. He made two more voyages across the Atlantic. On one of these trips, the settlers in Isabella made Columbus a prisoner and sent him back to Spain in chains.

On his fourth and last voyage, Columbus probably landed on the shore of North America near the place where the Panama Canal is now built. But he became sick and almost blind and had to return to Spain. When he reached home, he was not welcomed as the great admiral. Portuguese sailors had now found the way around Africa and had reached the real Indies. Portugal was becoming rich by trading in the East. Columbus had not succeeded in increasing Spanish trade. The king of Spain was jealous of the Portuguese and angry with Columbus for his failure.

Soon after the old explorer had landed in Spain for the last time, Queen Isabella died. Columbus himself did not live long after that. He always felt sure that he would find the rich trading centers of the East if he could only try once more. He

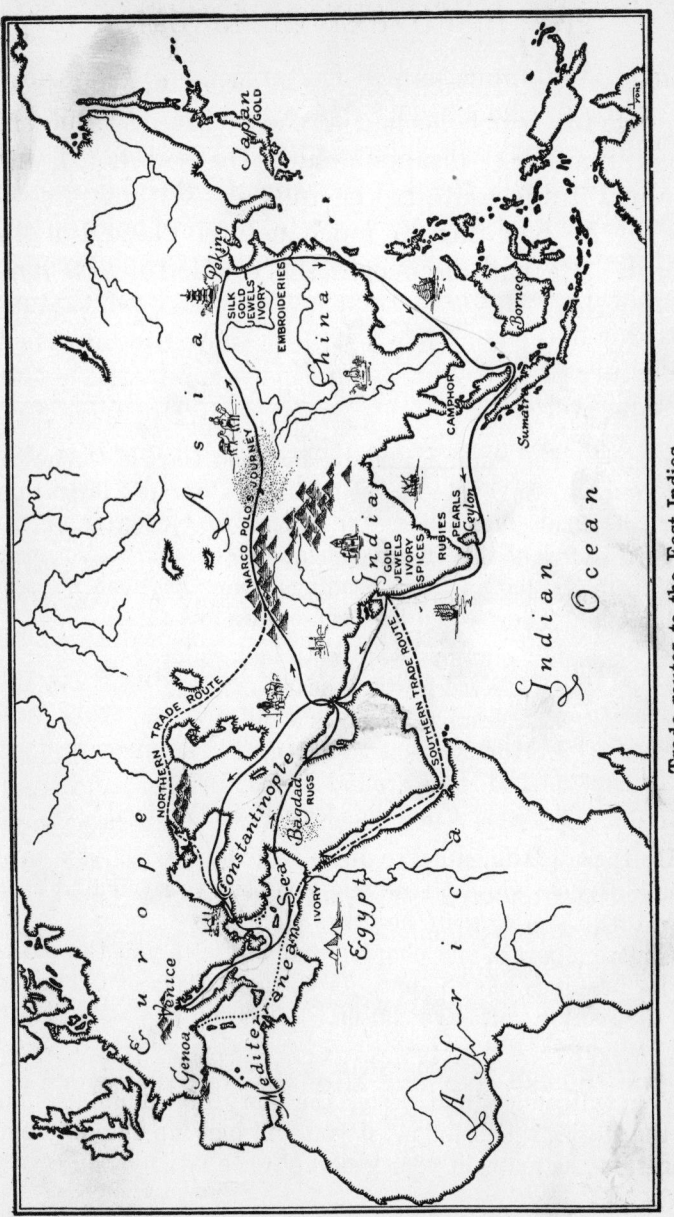

Trade routes to the East Indies

believed that the cities of gold were not far from the islands which he had already visited. But the great man died disappointed. He had not found the new trade route to the Indies. Without knowing it, he had done a much greater thing for the world. He had discovered the wonderful new land of America.

FINDING THE IMPORTANT POINTS

In this chapter you find several headings. See if you can find the most important points under each of these headings. For example: under **Boyhood Days of Columbus** you find why he wanted to be a sailor. You also learn that ships brought rugs, silks, and spices to Genoa from the eastern shores of the Mediterranean Sea.

You might put in more headings under **Boyhood Days of Columbus**. They would look something like this:

1. Columbus wanted to be a sailor
2. The stories they heard
3. Columbus becomes a sailor
4. How he went to Portugal
5. The route around Africa
6. What Columbus learned in Portugal

Do these headings help you to remember what you have read? When you are studying a lesson, you will find that it will help you to write headings like these.

Choose a part of this chapter that interests you the most. Write headings like the ones for **Boyhood Days of Columbus** for the section you have chosen.

USING A MAP

You will understand better the story of Columbus, and all the stories which follow, if you will look up the different places on the maps in your geography.

CHRISTOPHER COLUMBUS 19

Find on a globe or a map in your geography:

The East Indies — islands southeast of Asia
The Canary Islands — near the northwest coast of Africa
The West Indies — islands southeast of North America
The Mediterranean Sea   Asia Minor   Constantinople
Italy   Spain   Portugal

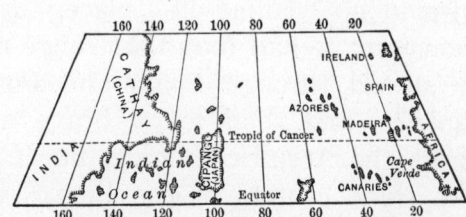

Where Columbus thought he was going

AROUND THE WORLD
Ferdinand Magellan

Exploring the New World

Columbus had sailed across the Sea of Darkness and had found no "falling-off" place. Instead of strange monsters, he had found a strange new land. The news spread through Spain and Portugal to other countries, and soon many brave men were sailing across the Atlantic, hoping, like Columbus, to find the trade centers of the East. But they found no beautiful cities with stores of spice and gold. Instead, they found only islands inhabited by savages, and the long shore line of a strange, wild country. The land was so large that people began to call it the *New World*, but most of the explorers felt sure that the New World was an unknown part of Asia.

One of the explorers who followed Columbus was an Italian named Amerigo Vespucci. He sailed for a great distance along the shore of South America and wrote many interesting letters about the country which he explored. People began to talk about

"Amerigo's land," or "America." In this way the new country received its name.

The letters of Amerigo Vespucci, and every true story told by an explorer, helped to make the Sea of Darkness a little less dark. Still there was much to learn and much to be done before the western route to the East would be clear.

Ferdinand Magellan

Two young nobles of Portugal stood in the entrance hall of the royal palace, waiting to appear before the king. Guards in brilliant uniforms stood at the door. Gathered near were several boys and young men, nobles' sons who were receiving their education in the service of the king.

One of the nobles spoke, and at the first words, the boys drew near to hear what was said.

"Have you heard any news of the exploring fleet lately returned to Spain?"

"That I have," was the answer, "and report says that they cruised among many islands and along hundreds of miles of coast without seeing a single city or palace."

"Then they did not succeed in learning any more than others have learned about that strange land?" asked the first speaker.

"No, and a strange land it certainly is. One of the captains went so far as to say that it is not a part of Asia at all, but a wild new continent; and that Asia lies beyond, much farther to the west."

"That might well be," said the first. "Portugal did wisely to stick to her own plan of finding a route around Africa to the East."

"Yes," was the answer, "and trade is growing every year. Already I have one merchant ship in the service."

One of the group who listened to words like these was Ferdinand Magellan. He had been sent to the court to be the queen's page when he was about twelve years old. A few years later, he was transferred to the king's service. There he heard much about the exciting discoveries in the New World and the dangerous voyages of Portuguese sailors who had found the way around Africa to India. The more he heard, the more young Ferdinand knew that he did not care to become a gentleman of the court. He longed for adventures on the seas. When he became a man, he left the royal court and sailed with a Portuguese fleet to India.

Young Magellan learned to know the rich East Indies. He cruised among the islands, visiting strange cities, exploring and helping to load spices. He became a good soldier and sailor, and fought many battles. Finally, after seven years, he returned to Portugal, having won honor but no wealth.

Magellan had always been interested in stories brought back by explorers from the West. Now more than ever he wanted to see these new lands. Why should he not make a trading trip to the Indies by the western route?

The same dream had led Columbus across the Sea of Darkness. Now Magellan could profit by the voyages of Columbus and other brave sailors of his time, and could start out with much more knowledge than Columbus enjoyed. Magellan knew about how many days would be required to sail across the Atlantic Ocean, and how large a supply of provisions would be needed for the trip. He knew something of the coast line of Amerigo's land (South America), and he knew that beyond it lay a great sea, which no doubt washed the shores of Asia. He felt sure that he could find a way either through or around the New World, and could go on westward to the Spice Islands, as the East Indies were called. There he would buy a rich cargo of spices, and then return to Portugal by the familiar route around southern Africa. He would sail around the world!

Magellan went to the king of Portugal to ask for ships and sailors. He told the king that the route around Africa was long, dangerous, and expensive. He also said that the western route which he was planning would be shorter and easier than the old way around Africa. You can see that he made the same mistake that Columbus had made. Both believed the earth to be much smaller than it really is.

He had been a page at the royal court in Portugal, and he had served faithfully in the Portuguese navy. But when he made a request for ships for his daring trip around the world, he was refused. Portuguese trade was steadily growing richer, and the king saw no reason for changing the route.

Then the young explorer asked, "Have I your Majesty's consent to seek aid from some other country?" The king answered coldly that Magellan might do as he pleased. As the disappointed sailor left, he knelt to kiss the king's hand, as all loyal subjects did. But the proud monarch drew his hand back.

Magellan was hurt and angry. Like Columbus, he left Portugal and went to Spain. The grandson of King Ferdinand and Queen Isabella was ruling in Spain and was willing to give him the ships which were needed.

The Voyage

Magellan was placed in command of five ships and about two hundred eighty men. Leaving a Spanish port, he turned his little fleet to the southwest. His plan was to reach the coast of America farther south than other explorers. The Portuguese ships had been successful in sailing around the southern point of Africa. If no strait or waterway through the American continent could be found, he intended to follow the Portuguese example and sail around the southern point of America.

The voyage across the Atlantic was rough and stormy, but the five ships safely reached the shore of Brazil and turned to the south. "Surely,"

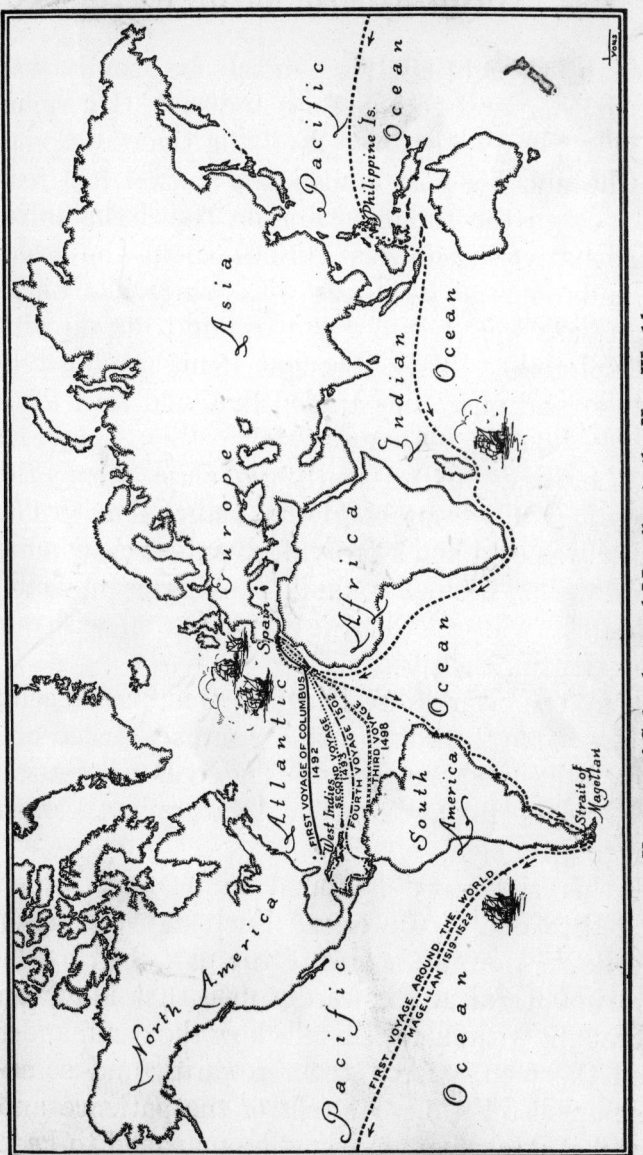

Voyages of Columbus and Magellan to the New World

Magellan thought, "there must be some way through this land to the East Indies." He sailed into every bay and explored all the rivers. Sometimes he and his men landed and looked for fresh food. Often the Indians came on board the ships, for the natives were very curious about the white men and their great canoes with wings like birds. The Indians were friendly and willing to trade with the explorers. They brought fruit and sweet potatoes, and once they traded five wild fowl for a fishhook.

Farther and farther south the ships went, the sailors carefully watching the shore line. The weather was cold and stormy, for winter was coming on. Magellan decided to find a safe harbor in which to pass the winter; then he would go on with his explorations in the spring.

When the winter set in, it was very cold. Troubles came thick and fast. Storms wrecked one vessel and injured the others. The food was getting scarce and beginning to spoil. Naturally the men began to grumble.

All this sad story is found in a diary which belonged to one of the crew. Each day the sailor wrote down the adventures of the party. He tells of the unfaithful and cowardly men that Magellan had brought with him. He tells how the commander coaxed the men, offered them rewards, and sometimes punished them. He tells of the patience and courage of Magellan, and how he managed to keep

FERDINAND MAGELLAN

in command even when the wretched men were rebellious.

He tells some very amusing stories also. Before the winter was over, some natives visited one of the ships. They must have been very tall, for the diary calls them giants. Their feet looked enormous because of the fur wrapped around them for warmth. The explorers called them Patagonians, meaning "people with big feet." That part of South America near the place where Magellan's ships wintered is still called Patagonia.

One of these giant men came on board Magellan's flagship. The sailors crowded around him and gave him some colored beads and bells. The man was a fearful sight with his painted face and rude clothing made of skins. He was so hideous that when he saw himself in a steel mirror, he started back in fright, stumbled over two sailors, and fell to the deck. The poor savage was so terrified that he fled and was never seen again.

For many weeks the explorers stayed in the cold but sheltered bay on the coast of Patagonia. They repaired their four remaining ships as well as possible. When the weather became warmer, they started south once more.

At last they reached a strait leading to the west. Storms and rough seas were met, but Magellan sent two of his best ships forward to explore. The two ships were gone for days. At last they came back with flags flying and cannons booming. They had found a waterway through the land to the western ocean.

Most of the sailors begged to go home. They said, "We have found the way, let us go back to

At last Magellan and his men reached a strait leading to the west

Spain. We may not have enough food for the rest of the trip, and we need new boats." The men on one of the ships deserted their leader and sailed for home.

But Magellan said, "We will go on if we have to eat the leather on the ships." So the three vessels which remained carefully sailed through the dangerous strait which is near the southern end of South

FERDINAND MAGELLAN

America. The strait is about three hundred twenty-five miles long. Rocky shores rise on each side. Only brave and skilful sailors could have passed through safely. The passage is named the Strait of Magellan in honor of the brave and determined leader.

On the Pacific Ocean

At last Magellan and his three battered little boats safely reached the great western ocean. It looked so calm and peaceful, after their stormy passage, that Magellan named it the Pacific Ocean.

Even the discontented sailors now felt that their hardships were over. They thought that in a few days they would reach the East Indies. Magellan did not dream that he was starting across the greatest open stretch of sea on the earth. Because of worn-out ships and scarcity of food, the rest of the trip was the most daring and difficult part of the voyage.

The sailors became hungry and sick. Twice they saw land in the distance, but they found only a barren island, on which there was not even fresh drinking water. The diary tells us that at last the sailors had to eat rats and sawdust, and even the leather from the ships. They softened the leather by soaking it in water; then they cooked and ate it to keep from starving. The suffering increased, and many of the sailors grew sick; a number of them died. Hardly enough well men were left to sail the three boats.

Finally, the starving explorers reached that part of the Pacific Ocean where islands are more numerous. They landed on the shore of the first one they reached, and to their joy found food and drinking water. The brown-skinned natives brought bananas

The brown-skinned natives brought bananas and coconuts to the ships

and coconuts to the ships, but they stole everything which they could carry away. Magellan, in disgust, called the islands *Ladrone Islands*, a name which means "thieves' islands."

With plenty of good food, the sailors began to get well. There was no longer any danger of starving.

FERDINAND MAGELLAN

A short journey brought them to one of the Philippine Islands. Here they landed and traded with the natives, paying for the goods they bought with the colored cloth, knives, mirrors, beads, and bells which they had brought from Spain. The king of the island was very friendly and promised to trade only with Spain.

Magellan tried to help the friendly king in a war against a neighboring tribe, but was killed in the fight. In another struggle many of the sailors were killed. The rest of the little crew were fearful and discouraged, but there was nothing to do but go on. There were not enough men left to sail three ships, so they burned their poorest one and went on to the Spice Islands in the two remaining vessels. One of these ships was not fit for a long voyage and was left here with its crew. The other started for home with a cargo of cloves, rich enough to pay the expenses of the whole expedition.

A long, difficult journey was still ahead of the weary sailors in the battered little vessel. Again they suffered sickness and hardship as they crossed the Indian Ocean and crept around the tip of Africa. At last they headed into the Atlantic for the long trip north to Spain. Almost three years after Magellan and his fleet had left Spain, eighteen sick, tired sailors steered their one remaining ship, the *Victoria*, into the port of Seville. The brave Admiral Magellan was not with them. But the great adventure could never have succeeded without this gallant leader. All the world agrees that the honor of making the first journey around the world belongs to Ferdinand Magellan.

Proof That the Earth Is Round

The old question, "Is the earth round?" had at last been answered. A small ship and eighteen men had sailed around the earth and had come back to the place from which it had started. Columbus had believed that the East Indies could be reached by sailing west. Magellan had proved that he was right. Explorers who followed Columbus claimed that America was a new world, not a part of Asia. Magellan's great voyage proved that this also was correct. Here were three questions about which men had argued and differed. Magellan's voyage answered them all.

Magellan's trip also added some new facts to man's knowledge of the earth. His journey proved that the earth is much larger than even the wisest geographers of that time had supposed. It showed that water covers a much larger part of the earth's surface than does land. Finally, it showed that the Atlantic Ocean, which had once caused so much terror, is only about one third the size of the great western Pacific.

THE ONE IMPORTANT THOUGHT

Sometimes a chapter or a section tells one thing that is very much more important than anything else. This is such a chapter. What do you think is the important thought in this chapter?

FERDINAND MAGELLAN

Write a paragraph about the one important thought in this chapter.

Draw on an outline map a trade route from Spain to the East Indies, around southern Africa.

Draw on this same map the route which Magellan took in sailing around the world. Be sure that you find the Strait of Magellan.

Find the islands where Magellan made his last fight for victory.

Monument to Magellan
This monument marks the spot in the Philippine Islands where Magellan was killed.

THE DISCOVERY OF FLORIDA
PONCE DE LEON

The Gifts of the New World

In 1929, Commander Richard Byrd and his men flew over the South Pole and drew maps of the land which they discovered. Each day, newspapers in the great cities published radio messages from the explorers. People read of their adventures and of the bleak land of ice and snow where they had made their camp. But no one thought of traveling to that cold region to settle and build a home.

In 1492 Columbus and his fleet sailed westward from Spain to find the trade centers of the East. In those days there were no radio messages to be published in daily papers. In Palos, Spain, friends of the wanderers waited and watched for months with no word to tell them that the explorers were safe and well. When Columbus returned unexpectedly, a strange story very different from Commander Byrd's was brought back to Spain. Instead of snow and ice, Columbus told of a beautiful land where the warm sun shone, birds sang, and flowers and fruit grew in abundance. This was the kind of place to which men were eager to go. The very next year fifteen hundred people went back with Columbus, many of them intending to make their homes in the New World. Columbus, himself, helped to build a small Spanish town on one of the islands of the West Indies. In a few years several towns were started, and many settlers were living on these islands of the New World.

At first the early Spanish settlers were disappointed with their life in the West Indies. They had expected to find rich cities where they could trade with the natives for silks and spices. The only cities seemed to be small Indian villages, but the soil was fertile and the climate was healthful. Many strange new fruits and vegetables grew wild. With Indians for workmen, the Spaniards soon planted large farms.

Seeds and plants were brought from Europe, and soon sugar, cotton, fruits, and vegetables from Spain were growing in the New World. There were also strange, new plants, corn, the potato, and tobacco that no one in Europe had ever seen. Soon the settlers found that these furnished some of their best crops.

Today cocoa and chocolate are known and used in most parts of the world. The first white men ever to taste this kind of food were Spanish explorers in Mexico. The Indians had cocoa which they used as a drink, just as we do today. The cocoa was made then, as it is now, by grinding the seeds of the cacao tree, a small evergreen which grows in Mexico.

The Spaniards were the first to bring horses and cattle to America, but they found here a wild fowl which had never been known in Europe. It was the turkey. Wild turkeys lived in many parts of North America and were hunted by all the early white settlers. When the first turkeys were taken to Europe, people were still confusing America with Asia. They thought that this strange new fowl came from Asia, the home of the Turks. It was therefore called *turkey*, and our famous Thanksgiving bird was named by mistake, very much as the Indians were.

The Spanish farmers in the West Indies prospered. They compelled the Indians to work in the fields as slaves, and they also brought Negro slaves from Africa. Many of the white men lived in great comfort on their large American farms.

But the New World was a place for adventure, and many a bold soldier was unwilling to live the quiet life of a farmer. Spanish governors, whom the king had sent to rule his new lands, were all eager to increase their power and wealth. The mystery of the unknown world around them invited every man to explore and conquer all that he could find. One of the Spanish governors, a man named Juan Ponce de Leon, was led to the coast of Florida by one of the strangest fairy tales that a man ever believed.

Juan Ponce de Leon

When Columbus made his second voyage across the Atlantic Ocean, Ponce de Leon sailed with him to seek fame and fortune in the New World. He belonged to a prominent Spanish family and, when a boy, he had been a page at the royal court. Later, Ponce de Leon became a bold soldier and fought for King Ferdinand and Queen Isabella in their war against the Moors. Then Columbus returned from his first voyage and brought with him a wonderful story of far-off lands. Many a Spanish adventurer wanted to sail with the great explorer when he made his second trip across the Atlantic. Ponce de Leon felt that he was fortunate to be able to go. The rest of his life was spent in the New World, and here he found the fame and the fortune which he sought.

When Ponce de Leon landed in the West Indies, he was strong, brave, a good leader, and a well-trained soldier. Such a man was sure to do well in this new land.

The Indians were very friendly when Columbus first came. But we have seen that they were often captured and compelled to work as slaves. Naturally they learned to distrust the white settlers, and trouble often arose between the Indians and the Spaniards. Ponce de Leon became a famous Indian fighter, and in time he was made governor of part of the large island of Haiti. Here he gained much land, owned many slaves, and lived comfortably in Haiti for many years.

But riches and power did not satisfy Ponce de Leon, for he was growing old. He thought with longing of the days when he was a poor soldier with an unknown world ahead of him. One day he heard of some Indians who said they knew where a magic spring of water could be found on an island far to the northwest. Anyone who drank from this spring would become young once more.

Ponce de Leon felt that youth would be worth more than all the riches of the world. Why should he not hunt for the magic spring? But first he must find the Indians who could tell him of this Fountain of Youth. He was soon successful, for this legend was well known among one of the West Indian tribes.

This is the story which Ponce de Leon heard. "Many years before, so many that the oldest men of the tribe could not remember the time, an Indian warrior and his squaw had grown old together. One day the West Wind whispered to the woman, 'Follow the trail till you reach the Fountain of Youth. There you may drink and be young once more.' They followed the trail and found a clear, bubbling spring of water. The woman filled a pearly shell and lifted it for the man to drink. In a moment he was again a strong, young warrior. When the wrinkled old woman had tasted the water, she became young and beautiful once more. Ever since that day they had lived happily, but once in every twelve moons they journeyed to the Fountain of Youth and drank together of its magic waters."

Ponce de Leon listened to the story with hope in his heart and asked many questions about the wonderful spring. The Indians said that it was located

The Indian warrior and his squaw drink of the Fountain of Youth

far to the northwest on an island called Bimini. The old Spanish soldier did not doubt that the story was true. We must remember that he lived in a time when people had just learned that they need not fear sea monsters and the "falling-off place." At that time almost anything seemed possible in this wonderful new land.

Ponce de Leon determined to find the Fountain of Youth and become young once more. He asked for the Spanish king's permission to explore the islands to the northwest of his home. The king consented; and, in March, 1513, Ponce de Leon started from Puerto Rico on his strange adventure. His three ships sailed toward the northwest until they reached the Bahama Islands. They stopped at many of the islands and parties went ashore to look for the spring. Some of Ponce de Leon's friends had come with him. They, too, were old enough to wish to drink of the magic water. How eagerly they tried every spring which could be found! They even bathed in the streams. Not one looked a day younger, but they still hoped that Bimini was just a little farther on.

Soon the three ships left the Bahama Islands behind and sailed on toward the northwest. At last Easter Sunday dawned. It was a beautiful spring morning, and a welcome sight met the eyes of Ponce de Leon and his men. Before them lay the coast of what they thought was a large island. On landing, they found huge trees and many beautiful flowers. The air was heavy with the fragrance of magnolia blossoms. Ponce de Leon named the place Florida, "the land of flowers." His hopes were high, for surely the magic water could be found

Ponce de Leon and his men drank from the spring

somewhere in this land of youth, springtime, and beauty.

The Spaniards landed very near the place where St. Augustine, the oldest city of the United States, now stands. Here they planted a cross and took possession of Florida in the name of King Ferdinand of Spain. The men were eager to explore, but the

Indians were suspicious, and Ponce de Leon took time to make friends with one of the chiefs and to ask for news of the Fountain of Youth. The Indians pointed to the west and made signs that a spring could be found not far away.

Eagerly the explorers pressed on. Travel was difficult, for the trees grew close together and heavy, gray moss hung thickly from the branches. But there in the midst of the forest they found a spring. It was a round pool, and at one side the water overflowed forming a small stream.

The Indians treated the place with great respect, as though it were a sacred spot. Ponce de Leon felt that here at last must be the life-giving water. He drank from the spring and his friends knelt down and buried their faces in the water. Then all waited; but their hair was still gray, and the lines of age still showed on their faces.

The disappointed old Spaniard turned away and led his men back to the ships. They sailed southward along the coast, stopping at many of the rivers and bays to hunt for the Fountain of Youth. Wherever they tried the waters, they met with the same discouraging result.

Perhaps other white men had already visited this shore, for the Indians seemed to fear the explorers. Sometimes they stole up when the ships were anchored and cut the ropes. Often they fought with the white men, and Ponce de Leon finally decided to go home. After rounding the southern

PONCE DE LEON

point of Florida and exploring part of the western coast, the ships sailed back to Puerto Rico.

Ponce de Leon Tries to Settle in Florida

Ponce de Leon was still an old man, but he had found a new part of this western world. He sailed for Spain to report his discovery to the king and to ask for permission to start a colony in Florida. The king was willing, but he first sent Ponce de Leon to conquer some fierce Indians who were making trouble in the islands south of Puerto Rico.

The sturdy old soldier went back to carry out the king's order. Several years went by before he was free to start his colony and to hunt once more for the magic spring of youth.

In 1521, Ponce de Leon and his colonists were at last ready to start. They took horses, cattle, sheep, and pigs, and landed on the western coast of Florida. The Indians were more unfriendly than ever. Soon they attacked the Spaniards and Ponce de Leon was badly wounded in the fight. When he knew that he could not recover, he said, "Take me back to Puerto Rico. The Fountain of Youth must be somewhere near, but I can never find it now."

So the little new settlement was given up and all the Spaniards sailed back to the West Indies. A few days after they landed in Cuba, Ponce de Leon died.

Like so many other great men, Ponce de Leon did not succeed in doing what he desired most to do,

THE DISCOVERY OF FLORIDA

but without knowing it, he gained lasting fame. He is the first man whose name is known who landed on territory which is now one of our Southern States. Through the adventures of Ponce de Leon the land which is now Florida became the property of Spain.

HOW WELL DO YOU REMEMBER?

Notice the subheadings in this chapter. The questions asked under each subheading will help you to remember the important points in the chapter.

I. The Gifts of the New World
   1. Make a list of the crops that early Spanish farmers raised in America.
   2. What new plants and what fowl did the Spaniards find in America?

II. Juan Ponce de Leon
   1. Tell the Indian story of the magic spring.
   2. Describe the search for the Fountain of Youth.
   3. Why did the Spaniards have so much trouble with the Indians?

III. Ponce de Leon Tries to Settle Florida

   Name the important facts about the explorations of Ponce de Leon.

Find the following places on the map in your geography:

Florida   Puerto Rico
Haiti   Cuba

SPAIN CONQUERS MEXICO

Hernando Cortés

The Desire for Gold

During the years which followed the discovery of America, many a Spanish boy listened to tales of adventure in the New World, and played at being an explorer. Among them was Hernando Cortés, who lived in a small town in the mountains of Spain. His father wanted Hernando to become a lawyer, so young Cortés went to a university to study. But books did not interest him. He kept thinking of adventure on the sea, and in the West Indies. Finally his father agreed that Cortés should seek his fortune in America.

The expedition which Cortés joined landed on one of the islands of the West Indies. The governor of the island, who had known young Cortés in Spain, offered him a large section of good land for a farm. But Cortés had very different plans.

"No thank you," he said. "I have come in search of adventure and riches, not to till the ground like a poor Indian. Just show me where gold can be had and I will fight for it if need be."

No one knew where to find gold at that time, so Cortés finally accepted the land. He became a wealthy farmer with many Indian slaves. He grew

SPAIN CONQUERS MEXICO

to be a good soldier, too, for there was much fighting wherever Spanish settlements were planted. The settlers often grew jealous of one another and quarreled among themselves. Sometimes they rebelled against their governors. There was trouble, also, between the Indians and the settlers, for the Spaniards not only made the Indians slaves, but they took from them whatever they wished without any thought of payment. Altogether, Cortés found plenty of adventure. But although he had gained some wealth, he had not given up his dream of finding gold.

All the early explorers, like Cortés, hoped to find gold and treasure in the New World. However, except for small amounts of gold on some of the islands, they had not yet found the riches they were hoping for. Sometimes they met Indians who wore golden ornaments. Where had the Indians found this precious metal? Somewhere in this new land there must be gold, much gold, and the white men were determined to find it.

One day a group of men came back from the mainland with a wonderful story that they had heard from the Indians. To the west, they reported, in the country of Mexico, lay a beautiful city with paved streets and bridges, temples, and palaces. This city belonged to a tribe of Indians called Aztecs, who dressed in gorgeous clothes and were so rich that they wore sandals of gold on their feet. The Aztecs were brave warriors and had conquered many of the Indian tribes who lived near them.

The Spaniards showed little surprise at this story. Ever since coming to America, they had hoped to find such a city. The word *gold* was all that was needed to make them start at once. The governor of Cuba lost no time in raising a small army to

The Indians brought gifts of gold to Cortés

explore and conquer Mexico. The Spanish soldiers took their muskets, a few small cannon, and fifteen horses. In eleven ships they sailed for Mexico, with Hernando Cortés as leader of the expedition.

When they reached the mainland, the Spaniards found hostile Indians. The natives soon learned that their arrows were poor weapons against the soldiers' armor, and that the white men's guns spoke like thunder and killed great numbers. The Indians came to Cortés, seeking peace. They brought gifts of gold, which delighted the Spaniards. Now they were sure that the stories which they had heard about this land were true. The Indians also brought some of their own captives and offered them to Cortés as slaves. Among these captives was a young Mexican girl named Marina. Cortés was kind to her. She became friendly toward the white men and stayed with them during the whole adventure. Marina learned a little Spanish very quickly, and was soon a great help in acting as interpreter for the soldiers. Through her they learned a great deal about the warlike tribes which lived in this part of the country.

Both Columbus and Magellan had trouble with cowardly men who wanted to turn back. Cortés had no such trouble. He and his friends planned a bold scheme. They told the soldiers that some of the boats were in bad condition, and might as well be destroyed since there was not enough time to repair them. A few days later more ships were sunk. When the soldiers began to complain, Cortés called them all together and said something like this:

"Brave soldiers do not think of retreating, and they care not what lies behind them. However, one ship remains. It has been saved for the cowards, who may now come forward and sail for Cuba."

Not a man moved. Instead, cheer after cheer arose for the bold leader. So the last ship was sunk. The soldiers could not go back. They had to fight.

The little army started on its march to Mexico City. On the way, the Spaniards often attacked the Indians whom they met. These natives were

The soldiers watched as the last ship was sunk

brave warriors, but when they heard the roar of the muskets and cannon, they lost all their courage. They had never before seen horses, which seemed to them dreadful monsters. They thought that the white men must be gods.

The Mexican Indians believed a legend which said that hundreds of years before, a white sun god had visited them and taught them many things. At last he departed toward the East, saying, "Wait and watch for me. I shall come again bringing many white gods with me. Then I shall reign forever in the city of the Aztecs."

It happened that Cortés landed in Mexico at the very place where the sun god was supposed to have disappeared. The Indians thought that the Spaniards were the white gods returned from heaven, riding terrible beasts and fighting with thunder and lightning. One tribe after another surrendered. Many of these tribes were old enemies of the Aztecs. They gladly went with the white gods to help them conquer the Aztecs' capital, Mexico City.

Cortés in Mexico City

In the beautiful city of the Aztecs, their emperor, Montezuma, knew all that had happened. Swift Indian runners had brought news of all that went on among neighboring tribes. Day after day Montezuma grew more alarmed, for these strangers were marching toward his own city. If this were the true sun god and his army, of what use would it be to fight? Montezuma sent messengers with every excuse which could be invented to urge the white men to leave the country. When these messages failed, he ordered costly gifts prepared, gold and silver dishes, and beautiful robes woven with bright-colored feathers. These gifts were sent to the white strangers with a great show of friendship.

The Spaniards could hardly believe their eyes when they saw the richness of the gifts. Certainly

HERNANDO CORTÉS

they would not turn back with things like this to be found and captured. They were even more surprised when they saw the beautiful Mexico City and learned how the Aztec Indians lived.

The Spaniards thought of the Indians as a savage people, living in huts instead of palaces. In Mexico, however, the Indians had learned to live well. The weather was always warm, and food could be had without much work. The Aztecs were never hungry or cold. They had time to learn a great many things of which other Indians knew nothing.

They learned to weave together bright feathers of tropical birds to make beautiful garments. They dug gold from their mines and learned to make it into ornaments to wear and into dishes to be used in their homes. They learned to build paved streets, bridges, temples, and great buildings. In many ways the Aztecs lived in as grand a style as any of the princes of Europe.

For their capital, the Aztecs had built a beautiful city on an island in the middle of a salt-water lake. Some of the streets were canals where canoes were used for travel. Three main roads led directly to the center of the city. Where these roads crossed the lake, great stone bridges were built. A huge tower stood in the center of the town, with many steps leading to the top. This tower was the Aztec temple where their gods were worshiped. At the top of the tower was the altar where the finest young men of the tribe were sometimes chosen and killed as sacrifices to the gods.

The houses in the great Aztec city were very large. Sometimes two hundred families lived together in one of them. The walls were made of stone, usually covered with white plaster, which made them dazzling in the sun. On the flat roofs of the houses grew palms and flowering plants. Here the people rested at sunset and enjoyed the beauties of their city.

Cortés and his army marched along the paved road across one of the stone bridges into the city. No one dared to stop them. Montezuma greeted the Spaniards as friends and guests. He gave them one of the great houses in which to live. To their surprise, it was large enough for the entire army.

Everything seemed friendly enough, but Cortés knew that he was really surrounded by enemies. He tried to think what he could do to make it safer to stay in the city. Finally he decided to try to get Montezuma into his power. He therefore sent a messenger to the Aztec chief, asking him and his brother to visit the white men in their house. The king did not dare refuse an invitation from the stranger who might be a sun god. He came, and although Cortés treated him as if he were a guest, Montezuma knew that he was really a prisoner, unable to leave the company of the white men.

Cortés Ordered to Cuba

One day the Aztec runners brought a report that more white men had landed on the eastern coast. Cortés had paid no attention to several messages from the governor of Cuba, ordering him to return. But now an army had come to compel Cortés to obey the governor's commands.

As soon as Cortés heard this, he chose a few of his best men and stole secretly away from the city of the Aztecs. Hurrying toward the seacoast, Cortés met and defeated the Cuban army. Then he talked to the defeated soldiers and told them of all the wealth which had been found in Mexico. He asked the captives to join his own army. They were more than willing to change leaders. Cortés marched back to Mexico City with more soldiers, more cannon, and more horses.

When Cortés reached Mexico City, he knew at once that something had happened. As he marched through the streets, they seemed dangerously quiet, and the market places were closed. The Aztecs did not try to stop the Spaniards, but they looked sullen and angry. As soon as the officer at the palace made his report, Cortés understood the trouble and knew that he had walked into a dangerous trap.

The officer explained what had happened. The Spaniards did not know that it was an Aztec custom to have a great dance in honor of their war god once a year. The time for this dance came while

Cortés was away. Great crowds of Indians gathered in the streets to take part in the celebration. The Spaniards were alarmed and thought that an attack was about to be made. They prepared to defend themselves by pointing their cannon at the crowd. This unfriendly action angered the Aztecs, and they began shooting arrows wherever a white man showed himself. Thus the fight started. The Indians seemed about to storm the palace and kill every white man there. But the Spaniards saved themselves by forcing Montezuma to go out on the roof and quiet his people.

Cortés wondered how long the Spaniards could defend themselves in the midst of the aroused and angry Aztecs. In the courtyard of the palace was a spring of pure water, and there was food enough for the present. But Cortés knew that they would soon need more food. He made the mistake of sending Montezuma's brother to reopen the market places. All that the Aztecs needed was a leader. They immediately called a council, which refused to obey a king who was held prisoner by the enemy. The council elected Montezuma's brother to take the king's place.

The Aztec Attack

Early the next morning the attack started. Aztecs swarmed all around the great palace, which the Spaniards had made into a fort. Once more the Spaniards compelled Montezuma to go out on the roof and talk to his people. But Montezuma was now no longer king. The Aztecs would not listen to him. They shot arrows and threw stones at the man who once had been their proud leader. One of the heavy stones wounded him. The Spaniards carried Montezuma to a safe place and treated his wounds, but the Aztec chief was broken-hearted. His people had turned against him, and he was a prisoner among enemies. He did not care to live, and refused to eat. A few days later he died. The news saddened many of the Spaniards. Those who had waited on the Indian chief were very fond of him, and many had still hoped to use Montezuma in making peace with the Aztecs.

The fighting continued fiercely, and Spanish cannon did great damage to the beautiful city. But the Aztecs had the advantage. They far outnumbered the white men, and they controlled the food supply.

Opposite the palace of the Spaniards towered the Aztec temple. It rose like a great house of blocks, each block being smaller than the one below it. Indians took possession of this tower. Whenever a Spaniard stepped out from the walls of the palace, a shower of arrows from the temple met him. The strangers were prisoners in their own fort.

The Spaniards knew that they must capture the temple. Twice they made unsuccessful attacks. At last Cortés strapped a shield to his left arm, which had been wounded. He chose his best men and Indian allies and led a third attack on the tower. The fighting was terrible, but the Spaniards pushed on. Up the steps they went, driving the Aztecs before them. There was no wall at the top of the tower to keep the fighters from falling over the edge. But no man thought of safety. Finally the temple was captured by the Spaniards. They destroyed the altars and threw the Aztec gods down from the tower.

"Now the Indians will be ready to listen to terms of peace," thought Cortés. He sent a message asking the Aztec leaders to come to the street in front of his palace. Cortés himself stood on the roof with Marina beside him to act as interpreter.

"You, yourselves, are to blame for this destruction," he said. "You have brought it on yourselves by your rebellion. But even now I will treat you well if you will lay down your weapons. If you do not, I will make your city a heap of ruins and will leave not a soul alive to mourn over it."

The Aztecs were not deceived. They knew that their own forces were far larger than the forces of the enemy. They knew that food was scarce in the palace of the Spaniards. They had surrounded the white men's refuge, and the bridges leading to the mainland were destroyed. Their own food was being brought by boats across the lake. There was no need to surrender, and Cortés was answered with a shower of arrows.

HERNANDO CORTÉS

The only thing left to do was to retreat. Cortés decided to leave the city under cover of darkness. The Spaniards built a movable bridge to be used in crossing the lake. They loaded each horse with golden treasure, and every soldier carried as much as he could. Great heaps of treasure were left piled on the floor of the palace.

One night when the streets seemed deserted and quiet, the Spanish army stole out of the palace. They hurried toward the lake, hoping to escape from the city. But the Aztecs knew that an escape would be tried, and they were waiting in canoes. As soon as the white men put their movable bridge in position and tried to cross it, the Indians attacked them from both sides. The Spanish cannon were of no use here, and the horses became frightened and jumped into the lake. A few Spaniards succeeded in swimming to shore, but many of the little army were killed or drowned.

When morning came, the sun shone down on a terrible scene of destruction. The Spaniards who had escaped fled toward the coast. Their weary leader got off his horse and sat on a rock as the soldiers passed before him. He rested his head on his hands and thought sadly of the failure of all his hopes.

Luckily for the Spaniards, the ships which had been sent to arrest Cortés had not been sunk as the first ones had. The Spanish leader was glad to find them when he reached the coast. But he did not think of giving up the conquest of Mexico. Instead of escaping in the ships, Cortés used them to send to a friendly colony for help. It was not long before help came — men, cannon, horses, and supplies.

Cortés Conquers the Aztecs

Once more the Spanish army marched to Mexico City. This time the Spaniards tore down the bridges and surrounded the city. The siege began in April, 1521, the same year in which both Magellan and Ponce de Leon died. For five months the siege continued. At last the Spaniards cut off the supply of fresh water from the city. The Aztecs could not hold out long without water. Before they gave up, however, they destroyed or threw into the lake most of the rich treasure of their capital. The cannon had already broken down the beautiful buildings. When the Spanish army at last marched into Mexico City, it was no longer the beautiful place which they had seen for the first time. It was a sad sight. The happy people had been killed and their city destroyed.

Although the capital of the Aztecs was in ruins, Cortés took possession of it for the king of Spain. Soon a Spanish city was built in its place, with a

HERNANDO CORTÉS

great church where the Aztec temple had once stood. Cortés became governor of Mexico. He made long exploring trips and fought many battles with the Indians. Gradually he conquered the country.

Shiploads of gold and silver from the mines of Mexico were sent to Spain. At last the dream of the explorers had come true. Here was treasure richer than any that had come out of the East. Here was wealth such as no king of Europe had seen.

STUDY HELPS

Choose the topic below that interests you most.

Read again carefully the part of the story which describes your topic. Then come to the front of the class and tell the other pupils all that you can about it.

1. The early life of Cortés in Spain and the West Indies
2. The Aztecs and their city
3. The story of the sun god
4. The march of Cortés to the Aztec city
5. The story of Montezuma
6. The capture of Mexico City

Find on the map in your geography:

    The island of Cuba   Mexico City
        The country of Mexico

SPANIARDS IN THE SOUTHWEST

DE SOTO—CORONADO—MISSIONARIES

Gold Makes Spain Wealthy

The news that Cortés had found great riches in Mexico spread quickly to the West Indies and Spain. Many men thought, "What other stores of wealth lie hidden in that strange land?" They decided to go to the New World and search for treasure.

About twelve years after the fall of Mexico City, a Spanish soldier named Pizarro led a little army from Panama down the west coast of South America. He traveled through the mountains of Peru and found the country of the Incas, Indians who were much like the Aztec tribe of Mexico in their civilization. The Incas owned rich mines of gold and silver, and their capital had even more treasure than Mexico City. Pizarro and his men would let nothing stop them in their effort to capture the Inca riches. They treated the Indians very cruelly and put the king to death. They captured the Inca treasure houses, with their heaps of gold vases, cups, plates, and ornaments; and they took charge of the rich mines of gold and silver.

DE SOTO — CORONADO — MISSIONARIES

Millions of dollars worth of gold and silver were sent back to Spain from Peru and Mexico. Spain became the richest nation in Europe. Now that so much gold had been found, Spaniards were certain that more lay waiting to be discovered in the New World. They sent out many exploring parties to search for the precious metal. Several of these expeditions explored the southern part of the United States. One of the most famous was the expedition of De Soto.

Ferdinand De Soto

One of the officers who had helped Pizarro conquer Peru was Ferdinand De Soto, a Spanish nobleman. Though he landed in the new world so poor that he owned nothing but his armor, he went back to Spain rich. The gold and treasures taken from the Incas in Peru made him one of the wealthiest men in Spain. He was bold and brave, a good soldier, and a leader of men. The king appointed him to be governor of Cuba, and *adelantado* (governor) of Florida.

Tales were being told in Spain about the great riches to be found in Florida. Several years earlier, a small Spanish army had been sent to explore and conquer it. Of three hundred men, only five lived to tell what had happened. One of these five returned to Spain and told exciting stories of the wealth that lay hidden in Florida, greater than any that had been found in Mexico or Peru.

De Soto offered to lead an expedition into Florida to find this great wealth and to conquer the country. Hundreds of men asked to join the expedition. Many Spaniards sold all that they had in order to share in the venture which would bring so much profit. Never before had Spain sent out an exploring party that was so large or so well supplied. There were nine ships, about six hundred men, and more than two hundred horses.

In May, 1539, De Soto was ready to start. The ships sailed into what is now called Tampa Bay on the western coast of Florida. Here the explorers landed and started to march inland. Whenever they came to a native village, they compelled the Indians to give them food. Often they burned the villages and killed the Indians or made them slaves. The women had to prepare the meals for the soldiers and do the work of the camp. The men acted as guides and carried the supplies.

Slowly the army moved northward through Florida, across Georgia, into South Carolina, and possibly into North Carolina. Then they turned westward to Alabama and Mississippi. Nowhere did they find gold. Nowhere did they find Indians who lived in the civilized manner of the Indians of Mexico and Peru. So cruelly did the Spaniards treat the savages whom they met that the Indians were in terror of the white men. From tribe to tribe went the news of the fierce invaders. Those who were able to get out of the path of the Spaniards fled. Many times they attacked the white men, and they made the march of the army much more difficult. When they knew that the Spaniards were looking for gold, they learned to defend themselves by telling false tales about gold to be found in the north or the west — anywhere away from their own country. So the Spaniards pushed on.

For three long years, De Soto and his men wandered through the wilderness. Many men and many horses died. The ragged army was now dressed in the skins of animals. The men lived on roots and berries and what they could steal from the Indians. The weary soldiers begged to go home, but De Soto would not give up.

Discovery of the Mississippi

Near the northern boundary of the present state of Mississippi, the explorers found their way blocked by a mighty river flowing toward the south. The Spaniards were probably the first white men ever to see the great river which the Indians called Mississippi, "Father of Waters." Even this broad river could not stop De Soto in his search for gold. The men built boats and crossed to the western side.

Month after month the weary march went on, through Arkansas, perhaps even through parts of Oklahoma and Texas. But now De Soto was giving up hope. This was the fourth spring since the great expedition had landed in Tampa Bay with such high hopes. If gold did lie in this wilderness, a man's lifetime might be spent in searching for it without success. The party turned back to the Mississippi and camped on the western bank near the mouth of the Red River. Here De Soto, worn out with the long marching, fell ill with a fever and died.

The Spaniards had told the Indians that De Soto was a child of the sun, and that he would never die. Now they feared to let the savages know what had happened; the Indians might attack if they knew that the Spanish leader was dead. The soldiers told their natives that the great commander had gone to heaven for a short visit with his father. Secretly, at midnight, they took the body of De Soto and buried it in the water of the great river he had discovered.

The rest of the little army followed the river to its mouth and there built ships and sailed to Mexico.

Coronado Searches for the Seven Cities

There were many strange stories told among the Spaniards in the days of exploration. Men were ready to believe anything, for had not gold and treasure more than any fairy tale promised been found in Mexico and Peru? A story led De Soto on his long search for gold. Another strange tale led Francisco Coronado and his men through the states of the southwest. This was the story of the seven cities of Cibola.

DE SOTO — CORONADO — MISSIONARIES 65

From a near-by hill Friar Marcos saw the city of white houses

This story told about seven rich cities far to the north of Mexico. In search of them, a Spanish priest, Friar Marcos, with a small party led by a Negro slave, Stephen, had traveled into the country we now call New Mexico. Stephen went ahead to prepare the Indians for the coming of the Spaniards. He came to Cibola, the first of a group of seven towns of the Zuni Indians. The Indians, however, did not like his rough, greedy ways, and killed the black man. When Friar Marcos heard the news, he dared not go into the town. From a near-by hill he saw the city of white houses

66 SPANIARDS IN THE SOUTHWEST

gleaming in the sun, and thought the place was full of palaces. This, he thought, must be one of the seven famous cities they were seeking.

Friar Marcos returned to Mexico without any farther search. He gave a glowing report of the city of Cibola which he had not been able to enter. The governor believed, like Marcos, that Cibola was one of the great cities of which the wonderful tales were told. He decided to send an expedition to conquer it, to find the other cities, and to bring back their wealth. Francisco Coronado was the leader of the expedition, and many of the wealthiest and noblest young men of New Spain (Mexico) went with him.

The explorers started from Compostella on the west coast of Mexico in the spring of 1540. They traveled northward into Arizona and New Mexico. When they came to Cibola and the seven towns, they found no palaces such as Friar Marcos had described. Instead, there were only white-plastered clay houses, called *pueblos*, several stories high. The houses were built on the rocky ledges of a steep hill, and were reached by ladders leading to doors in the flat roofs. The Indians lived very simply in these Zuni villages, and had no gold.

The Spaniards were disappointed, but they went on hunting for the seven cities. Coronado divided his men and sent groups in several directions to explore the land. One group reached the Grand Canyon of the Colorado River. Looking down that

DE SOTO — CORONADO — MISSIONARIES

great gorge they saw the river which seemed no larger than a silver thread far below. But since there were no rich cities near the gorge, the Spaniards were not interested in the discovery.

The expedition crossed the mountains and marched over the great plains where herds of buffalo roamed. Finally they reached the level prairies of western Kansas. Instead of rich cities, they found only wild Indians living in tents made of skins. Coronado decided to go back to Mexico. He had found no gold, no treasure, no seven splendid cities. Sadly the little army that had started out so gaily marched home. Months later the ragged survivors reached Mexico.

In his report to the king of Spain, Coronado said that the land they had seen was too poor for colonies. So Spanish colonists went farther south to Mexico and South America, where gold and silver might be found. For many years the land to the north was left to the buffalo and the Indians. When settlements were finally made, they were led by priests, not by gold-seekers.

Missionaries in the Southwest

Not less interesting than the lives of the great Spanish conquerors and explorers are the lives of the Spanish missionaries in the southwest. Most of these missionaries were born and educated in Spain. They came to Mexico and were sent from there to build mission settlements among the Indians.

With no thought of gold or conquest, these brave Spanish friars lived among the Indians, teaching them the white man's religion and the white man's ways of living. Usually the missionaries took with them from Mexico a few soldiers for protection and a few colonists to help in the settlement. Sometimes, however, they traveled and lived alone among the Indians. Many of these bold friars were killed. All of them suffered from cold, starvation, sickness, and poverty.

When a little missionary band found a good place for settlement, usually near a spring or in a fertile valley, they stopped. There they built a little church, and a house to live in, called a *monastery*. Around the mission buildings they put a wall, and outside the wall they started gardens and orchards or little farms.

Little by little the Indians learned not to fear the missionaries. Then many of them became interested in the Christian religion. They also learned better ways of farming and better ways of building houses and making clothing. When a family of Indians accepted the white man's religion, the family came to live near the mission and built a house outside the mission walls. In this way an Indian village gradually grew up around a mission. Many towns in Texas and New Mexico were once mission towns. Among them are San Antonio in Texas and Santa Fe in New Mexico.

DE SOTO — CORONADO — MISSIONARIES

Father Junipero Serra

One of the most famous of the Spanish missionaries to the United States was Father Junipero Serra, who was sent to California.

In 1768 two ships were loaded with food, seeds, furniture, and tools for farming and building. They sailed from the west coast of Mexico to the harbor of San Diego in California. Father Serra chose the longer trip and led a company of priests, farmers, carpenters, and soldiers overland from Mexico to the same place. At San Diego a mission and a fort were built.

Then Father Serra with some companions went farther north and established a mission and fort at Monterey. Bells were hung in the wall of the mission and each day they rang out an invitation to the Indians to come to the services. Sometimes an Indian would come near enough to receive a present, but most of them were afraid of the soldiers and their guns.

At last Father Serra decided that he ought to move the mission away from the fort. The captain of the soldiers objected, saying, "You will place yourself in great danger." But the priest said that he was not afraid that any harm would come to him from missionary work. The mission was moved near to an Indian village six miles away from the fort. Soon the Indians came to the mission. They lost their fear and allowed the priests to teach them the new religion.

70 SPANIARDS IN THE SOUTHWEST

The fearless priest opened the door of the mission

One night while Father Serra was away, an enemy tribe surprised the people at the mission. The friendly Indians living near the walls were first made prisoners. Then the warriors climbed the walls and set fire to the mission buildings. A fearless priest opened the door to speak to the savages and was immediately killed. A workman was also killed, but the rest of the mission inhabitants defended themselves through the night. At daybreak the Indians gave up the fight and disappeared.

DE SOTO — CORONADO — MISSIONARIES

When the soldiers heard of this attack, they vowed that the savages should be punished. But Father Serra was determined to return good for evil. He had worked many months to win the confidence of the red men, and warfare would destroy all his good work. Father Serra had his way. The mission was rebuilt, and the Indians never again attacked it.

Father Serra worked for many years among the Indians and established twenty-one missions. Today those missions have grown into such modern towns as San Diego, Santa Barbara, Los Angeles, and San Francisco. But although they were started by Spanish missionaries, Spain did not continue to hold the land, and these cities are now part of our own English-speaking United States.

Spanish America

Before the other countries of Europe had begun to plant colonies in America, the Spaniards had built many towns in the New World. Many thousands of Spanish men and women had left Spain to make their homes across the sea. Most of these Spanish colonists went to Mexico, to Central America, and to South America, for there gold and treasure had been found. There the Spanish language is still spoken and the people have many Spanish customs. The land to the north, now the United States, did not receive many colonists because it promised no gold or easy wealth. If the Spaniards had found gold in our country, the United States might have become Spanish, like Mexico. We might, even now, be speaking the Spanish language and reading our books in Spanish instead of in English. But the Spanish settlers went to the south, and our country was left to the French and the English to explore and settle.

MAKING AND ANSWERING QUESTIONS

Each pupil may take a paper and pencil and write one question about each of the seven parts of this story. A good question will ask for information about some important fact in the topic. It will also make a pupil think before he answers. A good question for the first topic would be: *What was the object of Pizarro's expedition, and what effect did this expedition have upon Spain?*

SOMETHING TO THINK ABOUT

Be prepared to answer any question you ask, and to answer further questions your classmates may ask you about your own questions.

Gold was lying safely hidden in California when Coronado was searching for the seven cities. If this gold had been found, what difference would it probably have made in the history of the Southwest?

Find on the map in your geography:

Peru, South America	San Antonio, Texas
Tampa Bay, Florida	Santa Fe, New Mexico
Mississippi River	San Diego, California
Colorado River	San Francisco, California

Bring to class any pictures that you can find of the country, cities, or missions mentioned in this story.

THE SPANISH ARMADA

SIR FRANCIS DRAKE

The Boyhood of Francis Drake

Not far south of London flows the river Medway. Before it meets the salty waters of the English Channel, the river widens into a broad and sheltered waterway. Here the great ships of the English navy used to anchor; and here, in the hull of a worn-out battleship, lived the boy Francis Drake.

As he played on the old deck of his boat-home, he saw the great ships at anchor or putting out to sea. His father was a minister who preached to the sailors of the fleet, and Francis himself was often with the sailing men, listening to the tales they told. Naturally, Francis wanted to become a sailor.

Francis Drake had to earn his living as soon as he was able to work. When he was about fourteen years old, he began to work for the captain of a small trading boat. He had to work very hard, but he learned to manage a boat and to be a very good sailor. The captain was fond of him, and several years later, when the captain died, he left the boat to Francis Drake.

Now Drake was captain of his own ship. Back and forth across the English Channel he went, and up and down the coast, carrying merchandise from one port to another. But he was eager to see the world. Before long he sold his boat and went on a voyage to the West Indies.

Drake Clashes with the Spaniards

He could not have chosen a better time in which to begin his adventures. Every year the treasure fleet from America came slowly home to Spain, heavy with precious cargoes. Englishmen longed for some of this Spanish wealth, and Queen Elizabeth encouraged them to trade with the Spanish American ports. But King Philip of Spain wanted to keep all the riches for his own country. He did not want the English to take any of the Spanish trade. He gave an order that English ships should not be allowed to enter a Spanish port. The bold English sailors paid no attention to the order. As a result, many fierce sea fights took place between the English "sea dogs" and the Spanish. The Spanish Main (as men called the waters near the West Indies) became a sea that was safe for neither English nor Spanish ships.

In such stirring times, Drake began his adventures with the Spaniards. Neither of his first two voyages to the West Indies turned out well. All the profits of the trade were taken by the Spaniards. Besides, Drake and his men had once been attacked by the Spaniards after the solemn promise of the Spanish admiral that they would be permitted to sail away in peace. In the fight several of the English ships were lost, and many Englishmen were made prisoners.

Drake grew to hate the Spaniards. He vowed that he would have his revenge. He would capture and destroy Spanish ships whenever he met them. He would take Spanish treasure wherever he could find it. When he reached England after his second voyage, he told Queen Elizabeth what had happened. She sympathized with Drake and approved of his plans. Though they were not openly at war, Spain was England's enemy. Queen Elizabeth was glad to have Drake do all that he could to weaken the Spanish power.

The Master Thief of the Western World

Drake laid his plans well. With a handful of men, in a tiny boat, the *Swallow*, he sailed again to the Spanish Main. In a small, unknown harbor, hidden from the Spaniards, he made his headquarters. For two years he learned all that he could about the Spanish ports and rich towns. Then, satisfied, he returned to England. Again he sailed for the Spanish Main, this time with two swift ships, ready to carry out his plans for revenge.

Whenever a Spanish treasure ship appeared, Captain Drake gave chase. Before the Spanish guns could open fire, the English ship was alongside.

THE SPANISH ARMADA

Brave English sailors climbed the sides of the treasure ship

Brave English fighting men were climbing up the sides of the enemy's vessel — a short, bold fight, and the Spaniards were made prisoners. The stores of gold, silver, and precious stones were transferred to the English ships.

SIR FRANCIS DRAKE

Again and again Drake was successful. If he found the Spaniards too strong for him, he quickly sailed away. Often he entered a Spanish port where treasure was stored. He surprised the people, carried off the treasure, and was safely away before anyone could stop him. In a short time the Spanish settlers in the West Indies and Mexico were in fear for their lives whenever Drake was known to be anywhere near. At last King Philip sent a message to Queen Elizabeth, asking her to stop this "Master Thief of the Western World."

For four long years Drake was kept at home. Many times he longed for the excitement and adventure of the Spanish Main. Many a time he remembered the great Pacific Ocean which he had once seen from the western coast of Central America. Some day, he meant to sail a ship upon that western sea. He knew that rich treasure could be captured there, for no English ship had ever visited that far-off ocean. The Spanish thought that they were safe in these waters, and their treasure ships sailed without guards. These ships carried gold and silver from the mines of South America northward to the Panama Trail. There they unloaded their cargoes of gold and silver. With much labor the great chests of treasure were carried overland along the Panama Trail (the same road now followed by the Panama Canal) to the eastern coast. There other ships were waiting to take the treasure to Spain. These ships which sailed across the Atlantic were

The great chests of treasure were carried overland along the Panama Trail

much harder to capture, for they were all prepared and watching for Drake. He resolved to visit the Pacific and capture the Spanish ships there.

Drake Sails on the Pacific Ocean

When Francis Drake was finally permitted to leave England, his plans were all made. Five ships were built, equipped with cannon, and supplied with everything necessary for a long voyage. Just where this fleet was going was a great secret, but Francis Drake, the finest sailor of the time, was in command. This was all that the sailors needed to know. They were willing to join the expedition.

When the fleet left port, it headed for the coast of Africa. From Africa it turned west and after a

SIR FRANCIS DRAKE

stormy voyage of fifty-four days reached the coast of Brazil. By this route the ships avoided the Spanish Main. Drake did not wish to be delayed by sea fights in this part of his voyage.

Then the fleet turned south and sailed along the same course that Magellan had followed almost sixty years before. Like Magellan, Drake had many difficulties. Storms so badly damaged two of the ships that they had to be given up. The other three ships sailed safely through Magellan's dangerous strait into the Pacific. There again bad storms were met and the little fleet became separated. One vessel was sunk; one, thinking Drake was lost, sailed back to England. Drake's ship, the *Golden Hind*, was blown so far south that it reached the southernmost tip of America. There the captain and his men looked out on the place where the Atlantic and the Pacific Oceans meet. No white man had ever been so far south.

Alone of the five ships, the *Golden Hind* remained to carry out Drake's great plan. Turning northward, he sailed along the coast of South America, to the Spanish settlement at Valparaiso, Chile. Here a treasure ship lay at anchor ready to sail to Panama.

The Spaniards had not heard of Drake for several years. They did not dream that any English ship would dare to come to that far-off coast. When the *Golden Hind* appeared, the Spaniards thought it was one of their own ships. They prepared to welcome friends. Instead, guns were leveled, and a rough English voice shouted to them to surrender. Almost before the Spaniards knew what was happening, "The Master Thief of the Western World" had captured their ship, and they themselves were prisoners.

With this rich Spanish treasure and plenty of food and fresh water safely stored in his own ship, Drake set sail for the north. The English sailors were gay and happy. There was no sickness and starving this time as there had been when Magellan and his poor men first sailed the Pacific Ocean.

At many settlements along the coast, the English sailors had what they called "good luck." Once, part of the crew landed and found a man asleep beside a heavy load of silver bars which he had been carrying.

"Excuse me," said one of the Englishmen politely, "but we will take charge of this silver for you. You can walk much easier without this heavy weight."

Another time the English sailors found a Spaniard and an Indian boy driving eight llamas. (The llama is a South American animal much like a small camel, and without a hump on its back.) Thrown across the back of each llama were two bags of silver which were being taken to the Panama Trail by land. The English sailors stole the silver, but the capture was too easy for them to enjoy it. They wanted excitement and adventure as well as riches.

When Drake reached Lima, Peru, he learned that a treasure ship had left for Panama two weeks before.

SIR FRANCIS DRAKE

Immediately the *Golden Hind* was headed on an exciting chase. On the way the British overtook and captured several smaller boats. From them they learned that the *Golden Hind* was gaining in the race. Every English sailor did his best, for each expected a share in the rich prize.

Drake offered a splendid gold and jeweled necklace to the one who should first see the Spanish sails. In a few days Drake's own nephew won the golden necklace. The Spanish prize ship was in sight, and the English sailors soon overtook and captured it. The cargo was transferred, and the *Golden Hind* was loaded till she could hold no more. From this ship alone Drake secured a great many jewels and precious stones, thirteen chests of Spanish money, eighty pounds of gold, and twenty-six tons of silver.

Sailing West to Reach England

Captain Drake now thought of the dangerous voyage back to England. It would be unwise to return the way he had come. Every Spanish ship along the coast would be watching for him. What should he do?

Drake decided to go north. He hoped that he could find a route around North America, just as Magellan had found one around South America. If he could not find a passage to the Atlantic, he would sail westward across the Pacific and so home, as Magellan's ships had done.

So Drake sailed north along the western coast of North America, exploring every bay and inlet in search of a passage. The *Golden Hind* went as far north as the island of Vancouver. Here the weather was so cold that Drake wisely decided to go no farther north. Turning south, he next landed on the shore of the present state of California near the Bay of San Francisco. Here he set up a post with the name of Queen Elizabeth carved upon it. Thus the land which is now California was claimed for England.

By this time Drake had given up the idea of finding a northern passage to the Atlantic. He decided to continue westward around the world. One day, when the wind was blowing right, the *Golden Hind* sailed boldly out upon the Pacific Ocean. Week after week the vessel held her westward course. At the Philippine Islands Drake stopped to repair the ship and take on fresh water and food.

The *Golden Hind* was badly battered, but she was able to bear her bold crew safely across the Indian Ocean and around the southern point of Africa. Three years after the voyage was begun, Francis Drake sailed once more into the harbor of Plymouth, England. His was the second ship of any nation and the first from England to sail around the world.

Quickly the news of these great adventures reached London. Queen Elizabeth was secretly pleased with her brave seaman, but she did not want to increase the anger of King Philip or cause a war with Spain.

SIR FRANCIS DRAKE

At first she refused to see Francis Drake, but soon she consented to go on board the *Golden Hind* and hear about the wonderful adventures of its commander. Drake served a great banquet to the queen. When the banquet was over, she asked Drake to kneel before her. Then she touched him on the shoulder with a sword and said, "Arise, Sir Francis Drake." So the "master thief" was made a knight of England.

Drake and the Spanish Armada

Very soon Sir Francis Drake had a chance to prove his knighthood. Spain was growing more and more angry with England, and England was growing bolder in annoying Spain. English "sea dogs" like Drake were capturing Spanish treasure and injuring Spanish commerce. English soldiers were helping the Dutch to resist the Spaniards, who at that time owned and ruled the Netherlands.

King Philip of Spain thought he could bear no more from the English. He made plans to punish the "English pirates," as he called them, and conquer the little island which dared to aid his rebellious Dutch subjects. So he ordered a great fleet to be built.

England knew how the fleet was to be used. In English shipyards also carpenters were busy, but they could not hope to make as many great warships as Spain could build. The people of England anxiously watched every move of their enemy.

THE SPANISH ARMADA

No one watched more closely than Sir Francis Drake. One day he disappeared from Plymouth harbor with thirty fast ships. A few days later he suddenly appeared in the port where the Spanish ships were being built. The English boats darted here and there among the great fleet that lay at anchor. English cannon tore great holes in the Spanish ships, and bold English sailors set fire to other ships. Before Sir Francis Drake could be attacked, he and his little fleet had left the port and were racing away on the open sea. When he reached England, Drake jokingly reported that he had been "singeing the beard of the King of Spain."

The damage caused by the daring English seamen to the Spanish fleet took a whole year to repair. England used this year to make ready for the coming struggle. Then the great Spanish warships were finished and the fleet sailed for England. The Spanish called their fleet the Invincible Armada, or "fleet not to be conquered." They felt sure of victory.

One day in the summer of 1588, the Spanish fleet of one hundred thirty warships came in sight of England. The ships sailed close together in the form of a great crescent. They had no fear of attack from the English. They intended to anchor in a French harbor. There they would take on board a Spanish army before sailing across the Channel and conquering England.

As the Armada approached, signal fires on the English hills burst into flame. Word passed quickly

SIR FRANCIS DRAKE

along the English coast. It reached Plymouth, where the English fleet was waiting. Quickly the English ships made ready and left the port, commanded by three brave admirals, one of whom was Sir Francis Drake.

Many a time Drake had captured great Spanish ships. The other commanders were glad to listen to his advice. Drake said, "The dog goes after the sheep, and not before them. Let them go by and we'll stick to them and pick up the stragglers."

The plan worked well. The English boats followed the Armada into the Channel. Sailing swiftly up to the Spanish fleet, the English guns fired several times while the great, clumsy warships of the Spaniards were turning to take aim. For several days the chase went on. Still the Armada stayed closely together and seemed as invincible as ever. It reached the port where the Spanish army was to be taken on board, and there it anchored to wait for the coming day.

All was quiet and dark, but the English sailors were not sleeping. Eight old vessels were filled with kindling, powder, and pitch. Then these vessels were towed close to the great Spanish fleet and set on fire. Suddenly there was one explosion, then another and another. The English boats burst into flames and drifted nearer to the great Armada. How could the Spaniards fight empty, burning vessels? They had to separate to save their own ships from the flames.

On board the Spanish ships was hurry and confusion. Sails were raised, anchors lifted, rigging became tangled, and each ship escaped as best it could.

The English sailors used their advantage well. They chased and fired upon the scattered Spanish warships. Even the weather seemed to be on the side of the English. The wind blew a gale, and a severe storm drove the Armada into the North Sea. The ships could not turn back, and had to sail around Scotland. Many of the ships of the fleet were wrecked on the rocky Scotch coast. Fewer than one third of the Spanish fleet ever reached home.

After this great defeat in 1588, Spain ceased to be the foremost nation in Europe, a position she had held for many years. Gradually England became greater and Spain grew weaker. Soon there was a new "mistress of the sea."

With the power of Spain broken, the English could safely settle in the New World. Before many years had passed, English colonies were growing up all along the coast of what is now the United States. No one had done more than Sir Francis Drake to build up the sea power of England. Without his work, the English colonies might never have been founded in our country.

SIR FRANCIS DRAKE

READING AND REMEMBERING

In school you learn to read aloud, and it is important to be able to do it well. But when you grow up, most of your reading will be done silently. Silent reading can be done rapidly, but not so fast that you fail to understand and remember what you read. Now that you have read the story of Sir Francis Drake, see if you can tell:

1. What made Spain a rich and powerful nation
2. How Francis Drake spent his boyhood
3. Why Francis Drake disliked the Spaniards
4. How he took revenge on the Spaniards
5. What King Philip hoped to do with his Spanish Armada
6. How the English met the Spanish Armada
7. Why this defeat of the Spanish Armada is important to us

From a port on the western coast of South America, follow a load of Spanish gold to the Panama Trail. How did the Spaniards take their gold from the western end of this trail to Spain? By what route would men today take a shipload of gold and silver from the western coast of South America to Spain?

Find on the map in your geography:

England	Lima, Peru	Philippine Islands
English Channel	California	The Spanish Main
	Vancouver	

ENGLISH IN THE NEW WORLD

JOHN CABOT—WALTER RALEIGH

John Cabot

Spain was not the only country to seek India by a western route. England, too, was eager for a share in the trade with those lands that Columbus said he had found beyond the Atlantic — China, India, and the Spice Islands. Five years after Columbus' first voyage, an English ship sailed westward to find China. In command was a skilful Italian sailor, John Cabot.

The ship reached the coast of North America near the island of Newfoundland. John Cabot went on shore and planted the English flag on the land he had found.

At the time of Cabot's voyage, Columbus had visited only the islands of the West Indies, and had not seen the mainland. So it happened that John Cabot landed on the North American continent before Columbus did, and the flag of England waved over American soil before the flag of Spain was planted there.

When Cabot returned, he told a strange story. He said that he had found the shore of China, but none of the rich cities of the East, nor any of the natives who lived there. He told of splendid fishing along the new coast, and advised English fishermen to go to the western land.

King Henry the Seventh of England was much interested in John Cabot's story. In the royal account book is a record of the reward the king gave the explorer. "To him that found the new isle, ten pounds." Today ten pounds is about fifty

John Cabot took possession of the land for England

dollars in our money. In John Cabot's time, it represented more than that, but still we would think the reward a small one for such a dangerous voyage. More than the reward of money, however, was the king's promise to send Cabot on a second voyage.

The promise was kept, and the next year John Cabot again sailed west. Whether he came to

America, no one knows, for Cabot was never heard from again. Then King Henry the Seventh died, and after him came rulers of England who were not interested in voyages of discovery. For almost a hundred years England did nothing to explore or settle the country which John Cabot had found.

During those hundred years, Spain was growing rich with American treasure. Stories of exciting adventures in America were brought back to Europe. The boys of England, like the boys of Spain, listened to the marvelous tales and hoped for adventures in the wonderful land across the sea.

Walter Raleigh

One English boy who listened to stories of the wonderful new land was Walter Raleigh. Walter lived in a big house in the country, not far from the sea. Sometimes guests came to the house, bringing news of what was happening in England and in other places. Sometimes, in a near-by seaport, Walter saw ships and the sailors who had visited the strange shores of the New World.

Walter liked books and study and so he was sent to college. But he did not stay in college long. When he was only seventeen, he joined a company of soldiers and went to France. Six long years full of adventure he spent in France. He came back to England a strong man and a skilful soldier, ready for more adventure. When Queen Elizabeth sent troops to help the Dutch fight against Spain, Raleigh

JOHN CABOT — WALTER RALEIGH

was with them. When there was trouble in Ireland, he was there. When his half-brother, Sir Humphrey Gilbert, sailed for the New World, Walter Raleigh was on one of the ships.

Of all his adventures, this voyage to America interested Raleigh most, for Sir Humphrey Gilbert hoped to start an English colony on the island of Newfoundland. Severe storms and a battle with the Spaniards compelled the little fleet to turn back before it reached America. Again Gilbert tried to found his colony, but on the return voyage from this second expedition he was lost at sea, and his plans for a colony were given up.

But Walter Raleigh was eager to carry on the work which his brother had started. After studying the reports of explorers, he decided that Sir Humphrey Gilbert had planned to locate his colony too far north. Raleigh himself fitted out two ships and sent them to explore the coast of North America between the island of Newfoundland and the Spanish settlements to the south.

The ships landed on the shore of what is now North Carolina. The men explored the coast for a short distance. They found the land so beautiful that they looked no farther for a good place to settle. When they reached England, they reported that the country was the "most plentiful, sweet, fruitful, and wholesome of all the world." The Indians, they said, were "most gentle, loving, and faithful, void of all guile." They named the place Wincondacoa

The Indians were very gracious to the colonists

because the first thing which the Indians had said to them was "Wincondacoa"—"What pretty clothes you wear!" Raleigh changed the name to Virginia in honor of the Virgin Queen, Elizabeth.

Walter Raleigh's Colonies

In 1585, Raleigh sent one hundred eight men to start a settlement in Virginia. The colonists landed on the island of Roanoke near the coast of North Carolina, and started the first English colony in what is now the United States.

These first English settlers found the land so beautiful that they called it the paradise of the world. But they did not want to work, as all pioneers in a new land must do. They built a few cabins but did not clear the land or plant gardens. Instead, they explored the country, lived easily, and waited for the supplies from England which Raleigh had promised to send. Their food was soon gone, and they took what they could from the Indians, who at first were generous and friendly.

In the end, the Indians grew tired of feeding the newcomers. By the time that a year had gone by, the red men were heartily sorry that these white men had ever come to their shores. The white men, too, were longing to be back in England, and grumbling because the supply ship from England had not come promptly.

One day the sails of an English fleet came in sight. Sir Francis Drake, the great English sea captain, was returning to England after capturing Spanish treasure in the West Indies. He had stopped to see how Raleigh's colony was getting along. The settlers were homesick and tired of their adventure. They needed food and supplies which Raleigh had failed to send. So they deserted their new homes and all sailed back to England with Drake. With them they took a few Indians and some tobacco, a product of Virginia, which was unknown in England.

A few days after Drake's fleet had sailed away, Raleigh's supply ship arrived from England. The captain found only empty cabins where the little settlement had been. But he did not want all Raleigh's efforts to be wasted, so he left fifteen men from his ship to begin the colony again. He gave them plenty of supplies and promised to send other men to help them. Then he sailed back to

England and reported to Raleigh what he had found and done.

Raleigh was disappointed that his plans for a colony had not succeeded, but he was not discouraged. He began to plan for another settlement to take the place of the returned colonists, and to join the fifteen men who had been left in Roanoke. This time he persuaded whole families to go, hoping the settlers would be less lonely and discontented in the new land if their wives and children were with them.

Late in July the ships carrying Raleigh's second colony reached Roanoke. The settlers found that the fifteen men left there the year before had been killed. The fort was in ruins and the cabins were destroyed.

But the settlers were not discouraged. Soon everyone was busy rebuilding the fort and the cabins and planting gardens. The children went into the forest and found all sorts of curious things to send back to their friends in England. The older people wrote long letters telling about their new homes. Most of these letters must have told the good news that a baby girl had been born since the settlers landed on the new shore. This baby was the first English child born in America. She was named Virginia Dare in honor of the new and beautiful land to which her parents had come.

Raleigh had appointed Mr. White, the grandfather of little Virginia Dare, to act as governor of

JOHN CABOT — WALTER RALEIGH

the new colony. All the settlers begged Governor White to return with the ships that were now ready to sail back to England. They wanted him to urge Sir Walter Raleigh to send more supplies as soon as possible.

Governor White hated to leave his people, especially his daughter and her helpless little baby, but he decided to go. The settlers agreed that if they left the island of Roanoke while Governor White was away, they would carve on a tree the name of the place to which they were going. If they were in any danger or trouble, they would cut a cross above the message on the tree.

Governor White did not know, when he sailed away with the little fleet, that three years would pass before he would again see the shores of America. When the fleet reached England, the whole country was working to defend itself against the great Spanish Armada. Every ship strong enough for a sea voyage was offered to Queen Elizabeth for the protection of England. Sir Walter Raleigh found it impossible to send help to the little settlement in America.

Finally Governor White was able to return to Virginia. As he and his companions drew near the place of the settlement, he watched eagerly for some sign of welcome from the colonists. But there was no one to welcome him. Every cabin was empty and deserted; every colonist was gone. Anxiously the men hunted for a message. At last they found the word "Croatan" cut on a tree. There was no cross above the name. Governor White was encouraged, for Croatan was an island where friendly Indians lived.

White wanted to go to Croatan, but the ship captain refused. Stormy weather was coming on, and the captain felt that he dared not delay his return to England any longer. Governor White could do nothing alone. Sadly he returned to the ship and went back to England.

Other vessels were sent to America. Men searched again and again, but no trace could ever be found of the lost settlers. What happened to the first English colonists in America is still a mystery. Men still wonder about the fate of the Lost Colony and of little Virginia Dare, the first English child born in America.

Sir Walter Raleigh had twice tried to start a settlement of homes in America. He had spent a great fortune of his own and was compelled at last to leave the work of colonizing for others to do. In spite of failure, his efforts had not been wasted. He had interested many people in the new land of America. He had made known to the people of England how fertile was the soil and how healthful the climate in Virginia.

Before Sir Walter Raleigh died, a town had been started at Jamestown, in Virginia. Raleigh lived to see ships bringing rich cargoes of tobacco and other products from the new land that he had attempted to colonize, to England.

JOHN CABOT — WALTER RALEIGH

MAKING AN OUTLINE

An outline helps a reader to understand and remember what he has read. An outline tells the main facts of a story in short topics. The most important facts form the principal topics and smaller facts are grouped under them.

After reading about John Cabot and Sir Walter Raleigh, you may make a simple outline of the story, using the titles of the three parts as your main topics. The outline will begin something like this:

I. John Cabot
   1. First English Voyage to America
   2. ----------------------------------

II. Sir Walter Raleigh
   1. Early Home
   2. ----------------------------------

III. Raleigh's Colonies
   1. ----------------------------------
   2. ----------------------------------

SOMETHING TO THINK ABOUT

What kind of work would settlers in the New World need to do in order to make a successful colony?

Find the island of Roanoke and the Roanoke River on the map in your geography.

What city is named for Sir Walter Raleigh?

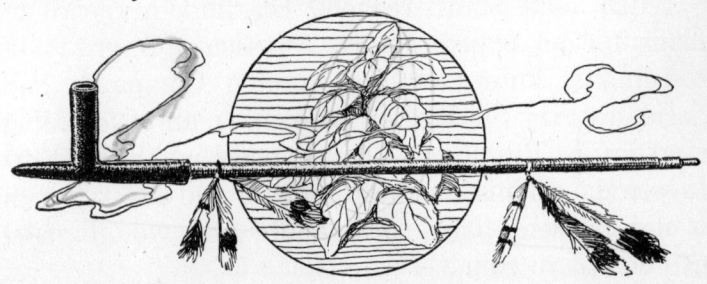

THE JAMESTOWN COLONY

Captain John Smith

Early Adventures

While Raleigh was trying to plant a colony in America and Captain Drake was capturing Spanish treasure, a boy named John Smith was growing up in England. Strong he was, and daring; and lonely, too, after both his father and mother had died. When he was only sixteen years old, he left his home to be a soldier. In France, in Hungary, in Turkey, and in other countries of Europe, he marched and fought. He was wounded; he was captured and made a slave; and he escaped and wandered over the great plains of Russia. At last he returned to England, an experienced soldier and a strong leader of men.

The First Permanent English Settlement in America

When John Smith reached England, he heard of plans for an expedition to America. A group of merchants, known as the London Company, had decided to try Sir Walter Raleigh's plan of founding a colony in Virginia. They hoped that in the New World the colonists would find gold and silver, which would be sent back to England and would make the company rich.

CAPTAIN JOHN SMITH

Captain John Smith was glad to join the expedition, and the company was pleased to send such an able soldier. One hundred four others were chosen to make up the little colony, but they were not chosen wisely. The colonists should have been men who could endure hardships, build homes, cut down the forests, and plant fields of grain. But of the one hundred five colonists, only twenty-three were workmen. One was a soldier, and the others were idle, good-for-nothing men who did not know how to do any useful work. Many of them felt very important and called themselves "gentlemen." They had wasted their money; some had even been in prison, and now they expected to find riches and adventure in America.

On a cold winter day in 1607, three small ships started across the Atlantic with the settlers for the new colony. A long and stormy voyage brought them to America in the early spring weather. In April the small fleet sailed up the coast of North America, looking for Raleigh's island of Roanoke.

Strong winds blew the ships farther north into a large bay. Glad to escape the stormy waves, the ships sailed between the two points of land which form the gateway to Chesapeake Bay. In honor of the king's two sons, the points of land were named Cape Henry and Cape Charles. After sailing a short distance up the bay, the ships came to the mouth of a broad river, which the settlers named the James River in honor of the king.

100 THE JAMESTOWN COLONY

The shores of the river were beautiful with spring flowers, green bushes, and large trees. The air was soft and warm. The colonists were happy that they had found such a beautiful place. They decided that here they would stay. After two weeks of searching for a good location for a town, the colo-

For two weeks the colonists searched for a good location for a town

nists started to build the settlement of Jamestown on a low, narrow piece of land between the James River and a great swamp. They thought that they could defend this place easily against an Indian attack.

There was much to be done. The forest must be cut and gardens planted, for food was already becoming scarce. Cabins must be built to shelter the men. As there were only four carpenters among the workingmen, the houses were built slowly. A few huts were put up and roofed with bark and grass. Some of the men lived in tents, while others dug holes in the ground for homes.

The settlers had brought with them a sealed box given them by King James. In the box were the laws for the colony, and the names of seven men who were to form a council to rule the colony. Captain John Smith was one of the seven named by the king.

The council of seven elected a president, but he did not know how to control the settlers. Soon there was trouble in the colony. Many men would not work. The weather was so hot that even those who were willing to work did not feel like making any effort. Others made matters worse by hunting for gold and getting into trouble with the Indians.

Things went from bad to worse. The damp, unhealthful air from the swamp and the lack of good food made many of the settlers very sick. Often three or four died in a single day. Before the summer was over, half the colonists were dead.

John Smith himself was sick, but he recovered and did what he could to help the miserable colonists. He divided the bad, moldy wheat and barley and gave each man one cupful a day. He stationed watchmen at night to guard the settlement. He made friends with the Indians and gave them hatchets and copper in exchange for food. He did his share of the work of the colony, and hoped for the time when he might learn more about the vast country of Virginia. Many times when the day's work was done, John Smith watched the sun go down behind the forest and longed to solve the mystery of that unknown land to the west. Perhaps one of the near-by rivers led to the western ocean. The great Pacific might lie just beyond the mountains!

At last cool autumn weather came to end the long, hard summer. The sick began to recover. The Indians gathered their harvests, and for a while the colonists were able to get plenty of food from their red neighbors. Every preparation was made for the winter.

Adventures with the Indians

Now men and supplies could be spared for a trip. Eagerly, Captain John Smith started to explore the country. With a few men in a small sailing boat he went a short distance up one of the rivers that flowed into the bay. Soon the water became so shallow that the sailboat could go no farther.

Most of the party were left to guard the boat. But Smith, with two white men and an Indian guide, took a canoe and paddled on up the river. The water grew more rapid and more shallow. Soon the canoe, like the sailboat, could go no farther. Leaving the two men to guard the canoe, the bold captain pressed forward on foot with the Indian guide. Before he had gone far, Smith was attacked

Just as the Indian warrior was ready to strike Captain John Smith,
Pocohontas rushed forward

CAPTAIN JOHN SMITH

and captured by Indians, and the two men with the canoe were killed.

In a history of Virginia which he wrote after he returned to England, Smith tells of his adventures

The Indians thought that the strange needle was some magic charm

with the Indians. We do not know just how true these stories are, but they are very famous. Smith tells how the Indians tied him to a tree and were going to kill him. He took from his pocket a compass and showed them the needle moving about under the glass. The Indians thought that the strange needle, which moved without being touched, was some magic charm. They were afraid to kill any man who owned such a wonderful charm. The captain was untied and taken to the Indian chief as a great curiosity.

In the village of the chief, a solemn council was called to decide what should be done with Smith. Powhatan, or the great chief, was seated in the council house. Near him were the Indian warriors, and farther back among the women was the chief's twelve-year-old daughter, Pocahontas.

When all was ready, the captive was led in. Powhatan knew that Smith was the only real leader in the white settlement. He was sure that if this man were killed, the whole colony of white men could easily be destroyed. The council decided that Captain Smith should be put to death.

Powhatan's tribe had the custom that any woman could claim a captive to take the place of a relative killed in battle. Little Pocahontas liked the white man. Just as the Indian warriors were ready to strike him with their hatchets, the girl rushed forward. She threw her arms around the white captive and claimed him for her own. So Captain John Smith's life was spared and Pocahontas became Smith's faithful friend. For some time Smith was kept a prisoner among the Indians, but finally he was sent back to his own people.

CAPTAIN JOHN SMITH

More Lazy Gold Hunters

Meanwhile, the colonists at Jamestown were doing much as they pleased. The work of clearing land for the next summer's harvest stopped. The food was not carefully saved and was rapidly disappearing. The storehouse was nearly empty.

One day when the men were discouraged, hungry, and quarreling with one another, Captain Smith walked into the settlement. The same day, a ship from England sailed up the river. What a happy time for the little colony! Here were more settlers from home, and a fresh supply of food, and here was John Smith once more among them.

The ship had brought scarcely enough food for the new settlers. Very soon the men were again grumbling over the small allowance of food given to them each day. But the Indians were not unfriendly and often gave the colonists corn in exchange for tools and beads. The rest of the winter passed without much suffering.

Captain Newport, who brought the new settlers, also brought a message to Smith from the London Company. He must find either the way to the Pacific Ocean or a lump of gold or one of White's lost colonists, or else he need not come back and show his face in England.

When Captain Smith received this message, he was angry. He wrote a letter which he called "my rude answer to the London Company." He described the hard work which colonists must do in order to live in the wilderness, and he told of the lazy men who had been sent out to do this work. Perhaps this letter helped the people of England to understand better the hardships of life in the New World.

The new settlers, like the first colonists, knew and cared very little about working. They had come to the New World to become rich, not to cut down trees and plant gardens. Scarcely had they landed before they set out looking for gold.

One day great excitement arose in the settlement. A man returned from a short exploring trip with his hands full of something heavy and yellow like gold. Every ax and spade was thrown aside while the men crowded around the man and plied him with many eager questions.

"Is it gold?"

"Where did you find it?"

"Let's go after some more."

Captain Smith examined the sample and knew that it was not gold at all. He explained that it was only a kind of iron, often called "fool's gold" because of its yellow color. He tried hard to convince the gold-hunting settlers of their mistake, but no one would believe what he said. All work was stopped and every man began to dig for the yellow ore. A ship was loaded and sent back to England with the "fool's gold." The settlers were greatly disappointed when they learned that the "gold" was worthless.

CAPTAIN JOHN SMITH

Smith Rules the Colony

During the second summer at Jamestown, Captain Smith made a long exploring trip looking for a water route to the East Indies. He went up the Chesapeake Bay and along the Potomac River. On another trip, he drew some very good maps of all the country farther north and wrote letters describing the land. He found and explored the Susquehanna River. Although he did not find a route to India, he did much to make the Atlantic coast better known.

During his long absence, the colonists again found themselves in trouble. From the first they had depended upon Captain John Smith for help and advice, but other men had held the position of president of their council. Now, with the captain away, the better men began to see the need of a leader who could control the settlers. When Captain Smith returned, these men elected him president.

In his history Smith tells of his struggles with the colonists. He tells of the rule which he made, that "he who will not work shall not eat." Of course, the idle "gentlemen" did not like the rule. However, when they found out that everyone must work six hours a day before getting any food, they quickly learned how to use an ax and a hoe.

In the spring of 1609, two years after the colonists had landed in Virginia, Jamestown began to look like a real settlement. There were twenty houses, a church. a fort with a well of pure water inside, and thirty acres of cleared land. The men were busy cutting lumber, making tar, soap, and glass. Captain Smith intended to have a supply of these products to send back to England by the next ship which arrived.

Slowly the colonists were learning how to live in the American wilderness. Slowly they were giving up their dream of gold, and turning to the work which would bring them comfort and happiness. Their greatest problem was how to secure enough food. Each year they needed to buy a large amount of corn from the Indians, for they had never raised enough for themselves.

Meanwhile, new arrivals were coming from England. As the number of white men increased, the Indians began to fear that their homes and hunting grounds would be taken from them. They decided not to sell any more food to the white men. They thought that the white men would have to leave the country if they could not get enough to eat.

The next time Captain Smith sent to an Indian village to bargain for corn, the red men refused to sell any. The wise captain knew that this was not the time to coax for food. He must show the great Indian chief that he had no fear. With about forty men in two small boats, Captain Smith went up the river to Powhatan's village. He asked for corn, but the chief refused. Knowing that Captain Smith would not agree, he said, "You can have corn if for every basketful you will give me one of your swords."

CAPTAIN JOHN SMITH

Of course John Smith refused to give up the swords, but he could and did compel the Indians to carry corn on board his boats.

The white men could not sail away until the tide was high. In the meantime, the chief plotted to attack the captain and his men after nightfall. When it was dark, Pocahontas quietly left the village and went to warn her good friend of the plan. A careful watch was kept. When the Indians stole down to the river, they were surprised to find the little band of Englishmen on guard. They pretended to have come on a friendly errand and gave up the attack. The savages soon decided that it was better to be friends than enemies to this brave captain.

Smith had among the settlers many enemies who did not like his methods of compelling everyone to work. They wanted Smith to go back to England. Besides, he had been wounded in the leg by a gunpowder explosion, and needed the help of skilful doctors. So, in the fall of 1609, Captain John Smith returned to England.

As winter came on, trouble began. Smith, as always, was greatly needed. No one else seemed strong enough to lead the colony. Indians robbed and killed some of the settlers. Work was neglected, and the food supply gave out. Some of the white men were too sick and weak to work. Many died. This terrible winter is known in history as the "starving time." Finally only sixty men were left from the colony of five hundred settlers.

THE JAMESTOWN COLONY

Those who were left decided to give up the colony and return to England. But just as they were starting for home, a ship from England, well supplied with food, brought help to the downhearted men. With a new governor to lead them and a large supply of food, the colonists decided to stay in the New World. So the Jamestown colony became the first permanent English colony in America.

Captain John Smith never returned to Jamestown, but he made several trips to America, exploring and drawing maps of the land from Maine to Long Island. He was the first man to call this part of our country "New England."

One day when he was in London, Smith heard that Lady Rebecca, an Indian princess from America, was coming to the city. To his surprise, he found that Lady Rebecca was his little friend Pocahontas. She had married a settler named John Rolfe, and had taken the English name of Rebecca. In England, Pocahontas was treated as a princess. She was presented to the king and queen at the royal court and everywhere was received with honor and kindness. A few years later Lady Rebecca died in England. Her husband, and later, her son, returned to live in Virginia.

John Rolfe was the first English settler to raise tobacco in Virginia. The plant which Raleigh's colonists introduced to England was by this time in great demand for smoking. Other settlers followed Rolfe's example, and soon ships loaded with tobacco

CAPTAIN JOHN SMITH

instead of gold were sailing to England. The tobacco trade brought to the colonists of Virginia the prosperity which the London Company had hoped to have from the discovery of gold. The colony that John Smith had served so faithfully became the oldest town in a large and prosperous colony.

FILLING IN AN OUTLINE

At the end of the last chapter you made an outline of the important ideas. See if you can fill in the missing topics in the outline of this chapter. Write the missing topics on your paper, numbering them as they are numbered here; for example, I. 4.

I. The First Permanent English Settlement in America
    1. The kind of men sent to America in this colony
    2. The work that must be done
    3. Troubles of the colonists
    4. _____

II. Adventures with the Indians
    1. Smith _____
    2. _____

III. More Lazy Gold Hunters
    1. A ship arrives just in time
    2. The message to _____
    3. _____

IV. Smith Rules the Colony
    1. John Smith's law
    2. _____ Indians
    3. _____

Find on your map of the United States:
    Chesapeake Bay   The Susquehanna River
    The James River   The Potomac River

THE PILGRIMS IN PLYMOUTH
MILES STANDISH
The Puritans and the Pilgrims

The second English colony in America was started by very different kind of settlers from those who first settled Jamestown. Instead of prisoners and lazy gentlemen seeking gold, the second colony brought to America men and women who wanted freedom to worship God.

They had not found this freedom in England. At that time, all the English people were expected to worship in the same way. All the church buildings in the country belonged to one church — the Church of England. Everyone was compelled by law to belong to this church and to pay taxes for its support.

Many people did not agree with the Church of England. Some of them wanted to make the services more simple. These people were called Puritans because they wished to "purify" the church. They believed that the people of England should live more simply, and should stop spending large sums of money on rich clothes, splendid furniture, feasting, and all kinds of pleasure.

Finally some of the Puritans said, "We will not have anything more to do with the Church of

England. We will separate from it and form a new church of our own."

King James was angry when he heard the ideas of the Puritans, and he persecuted those who held these beliefs. He was especially cruel to the Separatists, as those Puritans were called who separated from the Church of England. Since he would not allow them to hold their own church meetings, the Separatists met secretly to worship. In an old barn or in the home of one of their members, they prayed and listened to their ministers preach in the simple way which the Separatists thought right. Sometimes during a service the king's soldiers would suddenly appear. Then the quiet little meeting would be rudely broken up and the people arrested.

At last one faithful little group of Separatists decided to escape from the king's persecutions. They stole away secretly from England and sailed across the English Channel to Holland. These Puritans are often called Pilgrims, for a pilgrim is one who makes a journey or pilgrimage because he thinks that his going will please God.

The people in Holland were still fighting for their independence from Spain. They knew what it meant to be badly treated because of their religion. They were kind to the Pilgrims and allowed them to worship just as they pleased. The Pilgrims settled in the Dutch city of Leyden, thankful to be safe and free. In England they had lived in the country and most of them had been farmers. Since they did not own any land in Holland, they gave up their farming and became weavers, masons, and carpenters.

In spite of their freedom, the Pilgrims in Holland were lonely. All around them they heard a foreign language and saw the strange customs of their Dutch neighbors. The Pilgrim children went to Dutch schools and learned the language and ways of their Dutch playmates. This made the Pilgrim parents unhappy.

"We are English people," they said, "even if we cannot live in England. We must do something to make an English home for our children. Let us go to America. There we can live under the English flag, make our own laws, and worship in our own church."

The Pilgrims spent many hours in talking of this wonderful adventure and in making plans. Many stories were told about the fierce Indians who lived in that far-away land of America. How could the Pilgrims defend their new homes against the savages? Their men were brave, and all agreed that they could use their muskets when fighting was necessary. But a skilful soldier was needed to lead them. Some of the Pilgrims thought of Captain Miles Standish, an English soldier who had been helping the Dutch fight against Spain. Standish was not a Puritan, but he was very friendly to the English Pilgrims in Holland. They decided to ask Miles Standish to go with them to America.

MILES STANDISH

Captain Standish was quite willing to go, and his young wife agreed to make the dangerous voyage with him. A message was sent to London asking the king's permission to start a colony in America. King James promised not to interfere with the plans of the new settlers if they would cause no trouble in England. Then the Pilgrims persuaded some English merchants to lend them the use of two ships and the provisions needed for the long journey. They promised to send back to England shiploads of American products to pay their debt to the English merchants.

Sailing to the New World

At last a little company of brave men, women, and children were ready for the great journey across the Atlantic to the New World. In July, 1620, they went on board the *Speedwell* and sailed from Holland to the English port of Plymouth. There they were joined by friends in another ship, the *Mayflower*, and the two sailing vessels started across the Atlantic.

Both ships were small, and so old and battered that they were not fit to make an ocean voyage. Scarcely had they started for America, when the *Speedwell* began to leak so badly that both ships returned to England. Some of the passengers of the *Speedwell* were crowded into the *Mayflower*, making one hundred two passengers for the little *Mayflower* to carry. The *Speedwell* was left in Eng-

THE PILGRIMS IN PLYMOUTH

land, and in September, 1620, the *Mayflower* started again for America.

The little ship was tossed about by heavy storms and at one time was in great danger of being shipwrecked. Strong winds carried it much farther north than the Pilgrims had intended to go. At last, on November 20, 1620, a long sandy strip of land was seen reaching out like a friendly arm to protect the little *Mayflower* from the wind. Gladly the captain anchored his ship in the shelter of Cape Cod.

Thirteen years before, the first Jamestown settlers had sunshine and spring flowers to welcome them to the new land. But the Pilgrims found a cold, bare, icy coast with the dark winter sky above. They had no sealed box of orders from the king, but had to depend on themselves for everything. The men held a meeting in the cabin of the *Mayflower* and wrote the laws which were to govern their little colony. These written laws were called the *Mayflower Compact*. All the men signed the Compact, promising to obey the laws of the colony. John Carver, the oldest man, was chosen governor, and Miles Standish was made captain.

Choosing a Location for the New Colony

The next day was Sunday. The Pilgrims all stayed on board the *Mayflower* and listened to a long sermon from their minister, Elder Brewster. Early on Monday morning all went ashore, and some of the men worked on a small sailing boat which they wanted to use in exploring the coast in search of a good place to build homes. Miles Standish and others kept guard to prevent a sudden Indian attack.

For nearly five weeks the Pilgrims lived on the *Mayflower* while they waited for Miles Standish and a few chosen men to find a good place to build the settlement. The Pilgrims needed springs of pure water, fertile ground for their gardens, and a good bay where ships from England could anchor. The place must also be one which could be easily defended from Indian attacks. The weather was growing colder, and light snow fell. Before the winter set in, such a place must be found for the settlement.

Miles Standish and his men made two trips along the coast of Cape Cod but could find no spot suitable for the Pilgrim colony. At last they loaded the sailboat for a longer trip away from the *Mayflower* than had yet been taken. On the sixteenth of December, Standish and ten of the Pilgrim men started out again to look for a place for the settlement. The weather was so cold that spray blown from the ocean soon covered the men and the boat with ice. At night the explorers landed and slept on the ground around a big camp fire, while a careful guard kept watch for Indians.

One morning, as some of the men were cooking breakfast, the horrible sounds of an Indian warwhoop

118 THE PILGRIMS IN PLYMOUTH

came from the near-by forest. In a moment a shower of arrows rained down upon the men. Miles Standish quickly took command and soon muskets were answering the arrows. The frightened Indians turned and ran back into the woods. Later the Pilgrims learned why these Indians were

Soon muskets were answering the arrows

unfriendly. A few years before, an English captain had landed on this coast. He had captured some of the Indians and sold them as slaves in Europe. Now the poor savages feared all Englishmen.

One day the little boat sailed into a fine bay on the mainland. On the shore was a hill where a fort could be built. There were streams of fresh

MILES STANDISH

water and plenty of good land for farming. Some of the land was already cleared, and close at hand were sand, clay, and stone for building. At last the place for the colony had been found!

Eagerly the men returned to the *Mayflower* and told their friends about the fine bay and the good land. On the map of New England which John Smith had drawn the bay was called Plymouth. The Pilgrims were glad that their settlement in the New World would have the name of the great English port from which they had sailed. They were very happy when the *Mayflower* sailed into Plymouth harbor and they could all go ashore and see the place where they were going to make their homes.

Building Homes in Plymouth

The Pilgrims landed in Plymouth on the twenty-first day of December, 1620. At once the men began the work of building houses. All the work of cutting the trees, sawing the logs, and dragging the lumber to the place of building had to be done by hand. There were no horses and only the simplest tools in the colony, and the work went on slowly.

First they built a storehouse. There was very little food to put into the storehouse, so some of the families lived there while their own cabins were being built. Others stayed on the *Mayflower* until their homes were finished.

On a near-by hill the men built a cabin with a flat roof. On the roof they mounted three small

THE PILGRIMS IN PLYMOUTH

cannon to defend the settlement. Inside the cabin the Pilgrims held their church services. Every Sunday they marched up the hill to the church. Every man carried a Bible in one hand and a musket in the other, ready to protect his family if Indians should attack.

The first three months in Plymouth were hard ones for the Pilgrims. Sickness had already started before they left the *Mayflower*. As the days went by, men, women, and children became ill and died. Food was very scarce, and the bitter cold of the New England winter increased the suffering. At one time only six or seven men were well enough to do the work of the village and care for the sick. One of these was Captain Miles Standish, whose wife had been one of the first to die. Before the spring came, half the little colony had been buried in the Plymouth churchyard.

In April, the *Mayflower* was ready for its homeward voyage. As it sailed out into the open sea, the Pilgrims gathered on the shore and watched it disappear. They had suffered cold, hunger, and sickness for more than four long months, but not one of them would desert his new home and return to England.

Help from the Indians

One fine spring day an Indian walked boldly into the village. The Pilgrims all stopped their work, but before they could reach for their guns, the red man called in English, "Welcome, welcome!" The

The governor ordered the snake skin returned filled with powder and bullets

Pilgrims gladly made him welcome to the settlement. A small feast was prepared. The Indian ate the food and talked to the settlers. He used a few words and many motions, but he made them understand that his name was Samoset and that he lived farther north, where he had known some English fishermen.

After a short visit, Samoset went away peacefully, but in a few days he came again, bringing another Indian named Squanto. Squanto was one of the captives whom an English captain had taken to Europe several years before. When he finally succeeded in returning to this country, Squanto found that most of his tribe had died because of a terrible sickness. He was lonely and spent much of his time with the Pilgrims in Plymouth.

Through the influence of Samoset and Squanto, a great Indian chief named Massasoit came to Plymouth and made a treaty of friendship with the Pilgrims. Massasoit brought with him his brother and one hundred warriors. They were dressed in deer skins; their faces were painted red, white, yellow, and black; gay feathers ornamented their heads. Captain Standish and his soldiers had also prepared for the great event. They wore their armor, and as the Indians came near, they fired a salute in honor of their guests.

One of the Pilgrims laid down his musket in sign of peace and carried gifts to Massasoit and his brother. The chief also laid aside his weapons and with a few warriors followed the soldiers to a cabin which had been prepared for the meeting. There Massasoit and the governor of Plymouth solemnly made a treaty of peace, agreeing to be friends and help each other in case of war. These promises were never broken as long as Massasoit lived.

Unfortunately, this treaty angered another Indian tribe, enemies of Massasoit's people. One day, not long after the treaty had been made a bold Indian stalked into Plymouth and threw down before the governor a bunch of arrows tied in a snake skin. The governor ordered the snake skin sent back stuffed with

MILES STANDISH

powder and bullets. As plainly as words, this answer to the Indian challenge said, "If you will have war, we are ready."

The Indian chief was afraid of the white man's gunpowder, and called it "black magic sand." He would not keep it in his wigwam. He was afraid even to bury or destroy the powder and he sent it back to Plymouth.

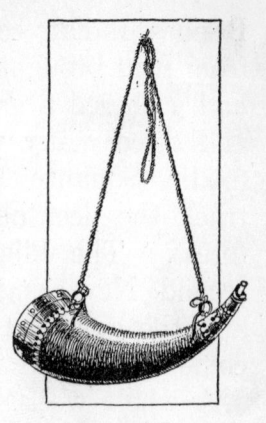

Many times the Pilgrims had trouble with unfriendly savages, but Plymouth was never attacked as many of the later settlements were.

Besides interpreting the Indian language to the Pilgrims, and helping them to make friends with the savage tribes, Squanto helped his white friends in other ways. He showed them where to get the best fish and game. He taught them how to use Indian corn. When the first planting time came, he brought seed corn to the village. He showed the men how to prepare the ground by putting a dead fish in each hole where the grain was planted. The fish made the soil richer and the harvest more plentiful. With Squanto's help, the first harvest in Plymouth was a success.

The First Thanksgiving

How thankful the Pilgrims were when the harvest was gathered. The storehouse was no longer empty.

Besides Indian corn, there were vegetables raised from seed brought in the *Mayflower*. The children had gathered a great store of nuts and had picked and dried many wild berries which were good for food. Squanto had shown the hunters how to track the deer and hunt the wild turkeys in the forest. The Pilgrims could look forward to the second New England winter with brave hearts, and the governor decided that the right time had come for a great feast of thanksgiving.

A whole week was set aside for this celebration. The first few days were spent in hunting. Deer, wild turkeys, and rabbits were brought to the village, and the women cooked the food. Corn and meat were also brought as presents by Massasoit and his warriors, who had been invited to the feast.

When all was ready, the food was spread on tables placed out of doors. For three days the white men and the Indians feasted and played games. Then the Indians returned to their homes and told the story of the first Thanksgiving feast to their families and friends. The news of the feast spread, and other Indians who heard of it wished that they, too, could be friends with the Pilgrims.

During the first year the Pilgrims could do little more than build their houses and provide food for themselves. But they had not forgotten the debt which they owed to the English merchants. The Pilgrims worked hard to repay the debt. They caught codfish and salted them. They cut lumber; and Captain Standish led many an expedition to trade with the Indians for furs. Each ship that came from England with colonists and supplies for the settlement was loaded and sent back with a cargo of furs, fish, and lumber. After six years of hard work, the debt was paid, and the Pilgrims all rejoiced.

Gradually the colony of Plymouth grew larger. Better houses were built, and many things were brought from England to make life in America more comfortable. Miles Standish bought a large tract of land north of Plymouth and built his house there. He called the place Duxbury, in memory of his old home in England. For thirty-three years he worked faithfully for the good of the colony of Plymouth. He lived to see thousands of English settlers come to the New World, and many prosperous colonies started in New England.

FILLING IN AN OUTLINE

Copy this outline on your paper, filling in the blanks.

I. The Puritans and the Pilgrims

    1. Ideas of Puritans and Separatists
    2. The king
    3. _____ Holland
    4. _____

II. Sailing to the New World

    1. Dangers of the voyage
    2. _____

THE PILGRIMS IN PLYMOUTH

III. Choosing a Location for the New Colony

    1. The search
    2. ----------------------------------

IV. Building Homes in Plymouth

    1. Hard work and dangers
    2. ----------------------------------
    3. ----------------------------------

V. Help from the Indians

    1. Samoset and Squanto
    2. ----------------------------------
    3. ----------------------------------

VI. The First Thanksgiving

    1. ----------------------------------
    2. ----------------------------------

Find the following locations on a map in your geography:

Cape Cod	Massachusetts
Plymouth	The New England States

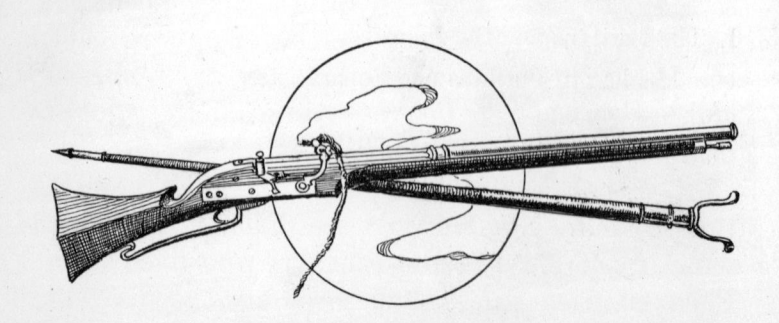

PROVIDENCE, RHODE ISLAND
ROGER WILLIAMS
Williams Disagrees with Puritan Beliefs

When the little town of Plymouth was eleven years old, an English minister named Roger Williams came to live there. The people of Plymouth welcomed Roger Williams, though he did not become their regular preacher. He worked as the Pilgrim fathers worked to support his family. He plowed and planted the rocky fields and cut the trees into lumber. Whenever he had a chance, he preached to his Pilgrim friends.

When Roger Williams arrived in New England, Plymouth was no longer the only settlement. Hundreds of Puritans had come to the New World since the *Mayflower* had brought the Pilgrims to Cape Cod. Along the Massachusetts coast they were settling in small towns. Boston and Salem had been founded. The new settlements were called the Massachusetts Bay Colony. Fishing, lumbering, and fur trading were beginning to make the colonists prosperous.

At first Roger Williams had planned to go to Boston, but he found that he did not agree with some of the ideas of the Puritans who lived there. Then he tried Salem, but there also he disagreed with the people. Even at Plymouth, where he finally settled, he preached sermons that alarmed the Puritans. He said, "You do not own this land you are using. The king gave the land to you, but he has no right to give what never belonged to him. This land belongs to the Indians. If you want to be honest, you must buy the land from them."

Williams said that everyone ought to be allowed to vote, whether he belonged to the Puritan church or not. He claimed, too, that people of any belief ought to be allowed to come to the colony without having to attend the Puritan church. These ideas angered the Puritans, for they treated anyone who did not belong to their own church just as they themselves had been treated in England. They said that everyone must attend the Puritan church, and that no one could vote in the colony unless he was a member of that church. When people with other religious beliefs came to Massachusetts, they were sent away. If they came back again, they were punished severely.

For several years Williams lived at Plymouth, working and preaching his new ideas. He spent much of his time with the Indians. For weeks at a time he lived in their villages in order to learn their language and customs. He always treated them so honestly and kindly that they accepted him as a real friend.

When the minister of the Salem church died, Roger Williams was invited to return to Salem. If the friends of the fearless preacher hoped that he would be careful not to anger the Puritans a second time, they were much disappointed. Roger Williams felt it his duty to preach what he believed.

The officers of the Massachusetts Colony became alarmed. What would the sermons of this bold preacher lead to if he were not stopped? The man was actually saying that officers of the colony had no right to punish people for not attending church. He was preaching that each man ought to think for himself even if he did not agree with the Puritan faith.

Finally Roger Williams was brought to trial before a court of the Puritans, and was ordered to leave the colony. This was in the month of October, 1635. The weather was already cold, and Williams was told that he could stay until spring if he did not "set about to draw others to his opinions."

Williams Is Forced to Flee

Roger Williams would make no promises, and before the winter was over, he was accused of disobeying this order. The Puritans decided to arrest him and send him back to England for trial. Friends of the young preacher heard that he was to be arrested, and they tried to protect him from the Puritans. He would have to leave the colony, they knew, but perhaps he could be saved from being sent to England.

One cold, dark night in January, 1636, a rap was heard at the door of the log house where Roger Williams and his family lived. The door was opened. There stood a messenger with a letter warning Roger Williams that the Puritans were about to arrest him. Williams was grateful to his friends for the warning. Leaving his home and family, he stole out into the wilderness to escape the Puritan officers.

Williams journeyed toward the south, helped along by friendly Indians. He traveled through the deep snow of the forest. He slept wherever he could find a little shelter, often in a hollow tree or under a pile of brush. He ate parched corn, acorns, and roots. Sometimes he lost his way and wandered about for days. After fourteen weeks of terrible hardship, he found the camp of Massasoit, the friendly Indian chief. There he was welcomed as one of the tribe.

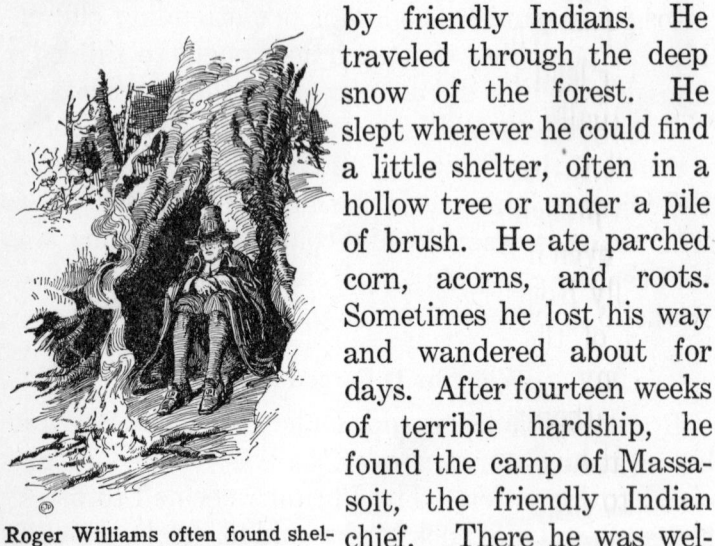

Roger Williams often found shelter in a hollow tree

But the Massachusetts Colony claimed this land where Massasoit's people lived. Williams could not be safe here, and he did not wish to bring trouble to his Indian friends. Again he started south,

After many weeks of hardship, Roger Williams found the camp of Massasoit

looking for the Narragansett Indians, who lived around the deep bay which we still call Narragansett Bay.

This tribe of Narragansetts were the same Indians who had sent the arrows tied in a snake skin to Plymouth. Roger Williams understood these people and could talk to them in their own language. They were glad to welcome him and to give him land on which to build his cabin.

The Providence Colony Started

It was now spring. Williams chose a place on the eastern bank of a small river and began to cut logs for his house. One day he was surprised to see five white men approaching. They were friends who believed just as Williams did and had followed him all the way from Salem. They urged him to start a colony of his own.

Soon they learned that the land on which Roger Williams was building his home belonged to the Plymouth colony. The new settlement could not safely be built there. So Williams and his friends traveled down the river in a canoe until they reached the head of Narragansett Bay. There on the western bank they saw some Indians standing on a large flat rock.

"What cheer? What cheer?" called the Indians, using the same friendly words which they had heard white traders call to each other as they met in the forest.

"What cheer? What cheer?" called the Indians to Roger Williams

Near "What-cheer" rock the white men found a spring of pure water. The beautiful country was just the place for a colony. Roger Williams bought the land from the Indians and started his colony. He named the place Providence, for he felt that God's care and providence had brought them safely to this place of refuge.

As soon as the colony was started, Roger Williams' family joined him in Providence. Then people began to hear that anyone, no matter what his belief, was welcome in the new colony. Many came to the new settlement, among them the Quakers, a peace-loving people who did not seem to be wanted anywhere. The Providence settlement grew into the present state of Rhode Island.

The little colony of Providence lived in peace and friendship with all its Indian neighbors. But the Massachusetts Bay Colony would not be friendly. Both Boston and Salem had very good harbors. Ships from England and the West Indies often landed at these towns to trade with the colonists. Fur traders and fishermen from all parts of New England brought their goods to Boston and Salem to be shipped. The settlers from Rhode Island also would have been glad to trade in Boston and Salem, but the merchants of Massachusetts would have nothing to do with the people from Rhode Island. The Rhode Island settlers lost much valuable trade because of these unfriendly Puritans.

Roger Williams Saves His Enemies

One day Roger Williams heard that the fierce tribe of Pequots was trying to persuade other tribes to join in a general war against the colonies of New England. He did not stop to think how unjustly the Puritans had treated him, but sent a messenger at once to warn them of the danger. The colonists were greatly alarmed. They knew that if the tribes joined together, the Indians could easily kill every white man in New England. The Massachusetts Colony replied in great haste, begging Roger Williams to persuade his friends, the Narragansetts, not to join the Pequots.

In this time of danger, Williams generously helped his old enemies of Massachusetts. In spite of bitter cold and stormy weather, he paddled his canoe across the freezing bay to the village of the Narragansett chief. Here he found that the Pequot warriors had already arrived, and that a great council of war was being held.

Roger Williams boldly joined the Pequot council

Inside the council house a large circle of painted warriors sat around the fire, and Roger Williams boldly joined them. Hour after hour the council continued, as the Pequots tried to persuade the Narragansetts to join them in a war against the colonists.

ROGER WILLIAMS 135

Finally, when night came, Williams wrapped himself in a blanket, lay down by the fire with the savages, and went calmly to sleep. He trusted his own Indian friends and showed no fear of the Pequot enemies. The warriors of both tribes could not help admiring such courage. The next day the council continued, and Williams used all his influence on the side of peace. At last, on the third day, the Narragansett chief told the Pequots that he would not join in their war against the white men.

Roger Williams had saved the settlers of New England, for other tribes had been waiting to follow the example of the Narragansett Indians. But the results were bad enough. The Puritans showed little wisdom in cruelly punishing the Pequots for trying to unite the Indian tribes against them. For a short time there was peace, but in later years the fear of Indian attacks kept the colonists in terror for many years.

Roger Williams' generous help at this time of danger made many of his old friends in Massachusetts ashamed of the way in which he had been treated. They asked the Puritan officers to allow Williams and all his colonists to return. But the officers really thought that they were acting for the good of their people when they still insisted that the teachings of Roger Williams were dangerous, and would bring ruin to the colony.

The small group of Rhode Island settlers grew in numbers and prosperity. More towns were built. People of many faiths came, and all were welcomed.

PROVIDENCE, RHODE ISLAND

Today the United States stands for the same liberty which Roger Williams gave to his people. But this small colony of Rhode Island was the first spot on American soil to prove that men can live together in peace and friendship even when they do not believe alike.

ACTING THE STORY

You like to go to the theater to see a movie or a play. How would you like to make a play of your own and act the story of Roger Williams?

Each pupil who takes part should say and do the things which he thinks these early people did. Of course, you will want to divide the play of Roger Williams into different acts or scenes.

1. Roger Williams in the church at Salem. Here one boy will be the preacher; others will take the part of the Puritans.

2. Roger Williams on his flight to Massasoit and his meeting with the friendly Indians.

3. Other people join Roger Williams in his new colony at Providence. You will want to put into this scene the naming of Providence.

4. Roger Williams in the council between the Pequots and the Narragansetts. Tell some of the things that Roger Williams might have said in this council of war.

THINGS TO THINK ABOUT

How did the products sent to England by the New England colonists differ from those sent by the men of Jamestown?

The New England colonists soon discovered that trade was a more profitable business to follow than farming. What do you know about the geography of New England which made this true?

Find on the map in your geography:

Boston, Massachusetts   Providence, Rhode Island

THE QUAKERS IN PENNSYLVANIA
WILLIAM PENN
William Penn Becomes a Quaker

A quiet little country town in the southeastern part of England was Wanstead. Many Puritans lived there; and there also was the home of wealthy Sir William Penn, Admiral in the Royal Navy.

Admiral Penn had to be away at sea most of the time while his son William was a boy. On his visits home, the admiral was pleased to see how much William had grown and how strong he was becoming. William was fond of all out-of-door games, and he could run faster and jump higher than most of the other boys. He was a good student, too, and his father decided to send him to college. Admiral Penn hoped that his son would grow up to be a well-educated gentleman, a friend of the great men of the country, and a leader in affairs of the government.

Young William Penn, therefore, went to Oxford University. For two years his record as a student was high. He was also a good athlete and rowed in the famous college boat races. Then, suddenly, he was expelled from the university and sent home in disgrace. What could have happened? After a talk with William, his father felt that the trouble could not have been worse. His son, for whom he had such splendid plans, had almost decided to become a Quaker.

The Quakers, or Society of Friends, were scorned and abused both by Puritans and by those who remained in the Church of England. They were thought of as a queer people who dressed plainly, never lifted their hats to anyone, and refused to fight. But the Friends had good reasons for their beliefs. They thought that all men were God's children, and therefore were equal and should be treated alike. They refused to lift their hats to a great man or even to use his title. They spoke to a prince as "Friend John" just as they did to the poorest servant. In the early days of the Quaker Society, the word *you* was used in speaking to important people; *thee* and *thou* were used in speaking to common people. In order to treat all alike, the Friends said "thee" and "thou" to everyone.

The Bible taught that all men should live at peace, like brothers in one great family. How then, said the Quakers, could it be right to fight for any cause whatever? The Bible also said, "Swear not at all," therefore the Quakers would not even take a legal oath in court.

The Quakers were constantly in trouble. They did not have churches, but held their meetings in their homes or even on the street. These meetings were against the law, and those attending them were often arrested and sent to prison. Becoming a

Quaker was almost certain to mean persecution and imprisonment.

Admiral Penn felt that his family was disgraced when William explained what had happened at Oxford. A Quaker had come to the university town and held meetings. Penn and a few other students had become interested in this man's teachings. As a result, they claimed that it was wrong to wear the bright-colored cap and gown of their college. They themselves put on plain clothes, tried to make other students do the same, and refused to attend the church services. Consequently the officers of the university sent the young men home.

The proud admiral was very angry when he found that William would not give up these foolish ideas. He would not allow the young man to stay at home. But Mrs. Penn secretly gave her son money so that he would not suffer, and before long she persuaded her husband to let William return.

Admiral Penn consented because he had missed his son; besides, he had thought of a much better way to tempt a young man away from the hard life of a Quaker. He suggested that William travel in Europe with the sons of some wealthy friends as companions. Surely, thought the admiral, life in the gay city of Paris would make any young man of spirit forget his foolish notions.

To please his father, young Penn began his travels in France. His father would not have been so much pleased had he known that his son was spending much of his time in a French college studying religion. William Penn was still trying to decide just what was right and true to believe. He had not forgotten the Quakers. In the meantime, however, he took fencing lessons, carried a sword, and dressed like other young men of the time.

When William Penn returned to England, the admiral was well pleased with his appearance. He sent his son to Ireland to help manage his large farms in that country. Surely there he would be safe from Quaker influence.

What a mistake the admiral had made! One day William Penn heard that the same Quaker whom he had known at Oxford was holding meetings in a near-by town. He went at once to hear the man preach, and soon afterwards he joined the Society of Friends.

Not long after this, William Penn was attending a Quaker meeting in Ireland, when officers broke up the meeting and placed the worshipers under arrest. When he heard the news, the admiral was very angry. He succeeded in having his son released from prison, but he could not force the young man to give up his religious beliefs.

WILLIAM PENN 141

The king smiled as he took off his own hat before William Penn

During the next five years, William Penn was often in trouble. Many times he was imprisoned on account of his speeches and writings in defense of the Society of Friends.

His angry father vowed to have nothing more to do with the stubborn young Quaker. But Admiral Penn could not help admiring his son's loyalty and courage. Quaker or no Quaker, William Penn had won his father's respect, and at last the two became friends again. Everyone liked the young man. He

142 THE QUAKERS IN PENNSYLVANIA

was on friendly terms even with the king and the nobles.

One day, when a company of men appeared before the king, every man except King Charles himself and William Penn took off his hat. Penn would not lift his hat even in the presence of the king. His Majesty looked at the young Quaker a moment and smiled. Then the king took off his own hat, saying, "Wherever the king goes, it is the custom for only one man to remain covered."

The friendship which grew up between the king and William Penn was a great help to the Quakers. But in spite of Penn's influence, the Quakers were still treated cruelly. Even in most of the American colonies they were persecuted and forbidden to build homes.

A Quaker Colony in America

William Penn often wondered how he could do more to help his poor comrades. At last he thought of a plan. Why could not a new colony be planted in America, a colony where Friends would be safe and free?

When Admiral Penn died, his Quaker son had been left with a fortune. The admiral's papers showed that King Charles owed the admiral a large sum of money. There was little hope of collecting this debt. The king spent a great deal of money, and he found it much easier to borrow than to pay. William Penn went to the king and offered to take a piece of land in America in payment of the loan.

WILLIAM PENN

This wild forest land across the sea had never cost King Charles a penny, so he was very glad to pay his debt with it. Besides, the land for which Penn was asking was not on the seacoast. The king thought that no other colonists would care to settle there. Therefore, Penn became the owner of a piece of land in America larger than all Ireland. Although Penn's land had no seacoast with a fine bay such as Boston harbor, the mouth of the Delaware River was deep and wide. Ships could sail directly up the river until they anchored near the land which Penn had bought. The purchase proved to be a good bargain, for this land is now the rich state of Pennsylvania.

The king was interested in the plans for a settlement of Quakers. He wanted to know what the colony would be called. People liked to use Latin and Greek names in those days, and Penn suggested Sylvania, a word which means "woodland."

"Call it Pennsylvania," said the king.

The Quaker leader objected. "I fear that it would be looked on as vanity," he said.

"Then call it Pennsyivania in honor of your father, the admiral," answered the king.

Thus the colony received its name.

News of these plans for a new colony spread rapidly among the English Quakers. "Friend William Penn," they told each other, "has fertile acres in America which he will sell so cheaply that all may buy. He will also help to provide a ship for the journey. Surely it is a fair and generous offer. Will thee think of going?"

William Penn was not content to help the English Quakers only. He sent letters to Scotland and Ireland, and he wrote to Germany, where people were also being persecuted for their religion. Everywhere this Quaker leader spread the news that in Pennsylvania any honest man would be welcome. Each could worship God just as he thought was right, and every citizen could help to make the laws and choose the officers of the government.

The first colonists were ready to sail before William Penn had arranged his business affairs in England. He sent his cousin to take charge of the colony for him. He also sent a letter of friendship to the Indians. William Penn believed just as Roger Williams did, that the land belonged to the red men, and he meant to treat them as fairly as he would those of his own race. The Indians, of course, could not read the letter. But when they were called together and someone who could speak their language explained what the letter meant, they were much pleased. This paleface chief, they felt, must be a real friend if he had thought of his Indian brothers before he had even seen them.

During the first year, twenty ships carrying about three thousand people sailed from Europe for Pennsylvania. Many of these colonists were English Quakers. Some came from Ireland and Wales. Later on many came from Germany to escape persecution there and to settle in a land of freedom. The German colonists were called "Dutch" by the other settlers. The "Pennsylvania Dutch" now living in Pennsylvania are the great-great-great grandchildren of these first settlers.

Many of the colonists settled along the river

The colonists landed on the western bank of the Delaware River. They had brought supplies and tools. Some even brought lumber ready cut for building their houses. But colonists came faster than homes could be built. For a short time the poorer settlers lived in caves dug in the river bank. As soon as possible, they cut their own timber and built houses on the land they had selected for their farms.

Penn Comes to America

In September, 1682, William Penn came to his colony in America. The voyage was hard, for sickness broke out on the good ship *Welcome*, and about

THE QUAKERS IN PENNSYLVANIA

thirty of the one hundred passengers died before reaching their new home. Finally the long, sad voyage was over, and the ship sailed up the Delaware River. A joyful welcome awaited the Quaker leader. All the colonists gathered to do honor to their governor.

William Penn was much pleased to find that they were already prospering in their new homes. He was delighted also with the land. The river valleys had fertile soil for farming; there were many woodlands for fuel and lumber; the rivers and harbors could be used for trade, and the climate was moderate, neither too hot nor too cold. Penn wrote in a letter, "Oh, how sweet is the quiet of these parts, freed from the anxious hurries and perplexities of woeful Europe!"

One of the first acts of Governor Penn was to invite all the Indian chiefs of neighboring tribes to meet together for a peace council. The story is told that he met the Indians in the shade of a large elm tree. There he paid them for the land which King Charles had already given him. The Indians understood at once that this white Governor was their friend and meant just what he said. They were pleased with the presents which he had brought them. The settlers and the Indians promised to live together in peace like brothers. They never broke their promise, and the treaty which they made has been called "the only treaty which was never sworn to and never broken."

WILLIAM PENN

When the solemn ceremonies were over, William Penn feasted with the Indians, and they entertained him with running and jumping matches. Although he was almost forty years old, Penn was still a young man, with the strong body of an athlete. He surprised and pleased the Indians by taking part in their games and jumping farther than any of them.

Penn's helpers had already chosen a place for a city. The plans for this city had been drawn in London, and even the name, "Philadelphia," had been selected. The name was made up of two Greek words which together mean "Brotherly Love."

The city was located on the bank of the Delaware River. When Penn arrived, some of the streets were laid out, forming square, regular blocks. As the forest trees were cut, they sometimes gave their own names to the streets which were to take their places. There were Chestnut, Walnut, Spruce, and Pine Streets.

On those streets today there is the constant roar of automobiles, trucks, and trolley cars. Once they were as quiet as a country road. In spring they were muddy, and in summer they were overgrown with grass. At milking time on a summer evening the cows wandered up the streets from their pasture. In winter the only sounds were sleigh bells and the shouts of boys throwing snowballs. Indians wrapped in deer skins often visited the town, bringing venison and furs to be sold to the Quakers in exchange for beads and trinkets.

148 THE QUAKERS IN PENNSYLVANIA

From the first, Philadelphia grew rapidly. In three years there were twenty-five hundred people living there. For many years it was the largest city in America.

William Penn could not stay long in his American colony. Business took him to England, where he remained for many years. He visited his colony only once again, but the laws of Pennsylvania were so just and good that the colony grew and prospered even without its leader.

Both in England and in America, William Penn spent his time, efforts, and money helping to bring justice to all. He had done a hero's work in the cause of peace and freedom. We are glad that his name will live in the name of the great state of Pennsylvania.

ASKING AND ANSWERING QUESTIONS

There are three subheadings in this chapter:
  I. William Penn Becomes a Quaker
  II. A Quaker Colony in America
  III. Penn Comes to America

Choose the one of these topics that interests you most. Read over the section of the chapter following the topic you have chosen.

Now write three or four questions on your topic. If you will turn back to page 97, you will see how questions may be made that will call out the important thoughts in a section.

Stand before the class and answer your own questions.

Find on the map in your geography:
  Delaware River   The State of Pennsylvania
          Philadelphia

THE NORTHWEST PASSAGE
Henry Hudson
Seeking New Routes

When we read history, we must try to think of conditions that are very different from those of today. We cross the Atlantic Ocean in less than a week. Our ship sends and receives radio messages every day. At home our newspapers tell us every morning of happenings all over the world. You remember that, while Admiral Byrd was near the South Pole, he told the world everything that was happening day by day.

But during the first hundred years after Columbus sailed across the Sea of Darkness, comparatively little was really known about America. Magellan and Drake had sailed around the world. This proved two things; that the world was round and that the continent of America lay on the western route between Europe and Asia.

Gold and treasure from the new land had made Spain rich, but the other countries of Europe did not share in this wealth. To them, America was a great wall blocking the way to China and India. Trading ships still made the long trip to the East by going around the southern point of Africa. Surely, men thought, there must be a shorter way. Perhaps a passage could be found through North America that would lead directly to the western ocean and so to China. If no passage led *through* North America, then without doubt one led *around* the northern end of the continent, as Magellan's straits do at the south. Somewhere through the New World there must be a northwest passage. The search for this Northwest Passage went on for years. Many explorers went out to hunt for it.

In England, a group of merchants, called the Muscovy Company, decided to explore for a new route to China. Not the Northwest Passage, but a northeast passage around Europe and Asia was to be sought. The company chose Henry Hudson, a bold and skilful sailor, to lead the expedition.

Henry Hudson

A few months before the first colonists started for Jamestown, Henry Hudson sailed from England for the Arctic seas. On board his tiny ship were his son John and a crew of ten men. With these he hoped to find a route to China through the icy waters north of Europe. Straight across the North Pole he planned to sail his little ship.

Hudson sailed along the eastern shores of Greenland until ice blocked his path. Then he turned east and explored the waters around the island of Spitzbergen. The sailors saw great icebergs, and in

HENRY HUDSON

a sheltered bay on the island they found many whales. The great creatures were playing in the cold waters of the bay. One of the whales dived under the boat. The sailors were afraid that the boat would be upset, but the whale came up on the other side of the boat without doing any harm.

For several weeks Hudson cruised among the islands of the Arctic Ocean without finding a passage to the Pacific. Finally ice and bad weather forced him to return to England. The following year he sailed again for the Muscovy Company. This time he went as far as Nova Zembla, an island north of Russia. Again thick ice and stormy weather forced him to return to England without finding the passage to China.

The men of the Muscovy Company were disappointed that Hudson had again failed to find the passage. They would not send him out on a third trip. So Henry Hudson had to look for help from other men.

In the kingdom of the Netherlands was the wealthy Dutch East India Company. For several years the company had carried on a rich trade in spices, tea, and rare silks. The men of the company felt that a route to the East shorter than the long way around Africa would help their trade. If there was a route by the northern seas, the company wished to have control of it. They were glad to hire Henry Hudson to make explorations for them.

The Journey of the *Half Moon*

Not long before this, Hudson had received a letter and maps from his friend, Captain John Smith. The letter told of the exploring trips which Smith had made along the coast of Virginia. On one of the maps, Captain Smith had marked a place where he believed a waterway to the Pacific might be found. This news from his old friend made Henry Hudson long to explore the place marked on John Smith's map. Some day he hoped to sail into the Northwest Passage and reach the great ocean on the other side of America. The Dutch Company, however, thought that the northeast passage around Europe and Asia would be easier. They ordered Hudson "to think of discovering no other routes or passages except the route around the north side of Nova Zembla."

The company's order must be obeyed; so Hudson sailed again for Nova Zembla. He started on this third exploring trip to the north in April, 1609, sailing from Amsterdam in a small Dutch boat named the *Half Moon*. More than a month later, he reached the most northern point of Norway.

In spite of cold and foggy weather, the *Half Moon* plowed boldly into the Arctic Ocean. Soon, however, Hudson was stopped by great, drifting icebergs. The sailors suffered from the severe cold. They grew discontented and hard to manage. They even threatened to take command of the ship and sail for home. What was to be done? Giving up

HENRY HUDSON

would be worse than disobeying orders, thought Hudson, so he tried to compromise with them.

Hudson Sails to America

He called the little crew together. Then he suggested sailing to America and asked their advice about changing the course. Every man was in favor of the new plan. Gladly the *Half Moon* was turned about and sailed toward the west.

The voyage across the Atlantic was very stormy. The *Half Moon* lost a mast, and her sails were badly torn. After many weeks, Hudson reached Penobscot Bay on the coast of Maine. Here he stayed long enough to repair his battered little ship. Then he turned south.

Late in the summer of 1609, the *Half Moon* sailed down the coast of North America, looking for a waterway to the western ocean. At last the little ship reached a part of the coast which Hudson felt sure was near Captain John Smith's settlement in Virginia. Hudson thought that he must have missed the opening through America, so he turned north and at last came to the fine broad bay which we now know as New York Harbor. The *Half Moon* sailed up the bay and anchored near an island called by the Indians "Manhattan" — "island of the hills."

When the Indians saw Hudson's boat, they were very curious. A party of them paddled out in their canoes to see the strange ship with its white sails. The mate of the *Half Moon* kept a journal in which he wrote down all that happened on the voyage. This is what he said about the Indians: "This day the people of the country came aboard of us, seeming very glad of our comming, and brought greene tobacco, and gave us of it for knives and beads. They goe in deere skins loose, well dressed. They have yellow copper. They desire cloathes, and are very civill. They have a great store of maize or Indian wheate, whereof they make good bread. The country is full of great tall oakes."

Manhattan Island and the land about the bay were very beautiful, but Hudson was hunting for a waterway leading to the Pacific Ocean. There before him, where the river which we now call the Hudson empties into the bay, a wide stretch of water extended far into the land. Perhaps this was the very opening about which Captain John Smith had written. Perhaps this was the Northwest Passage!

With high hopes Henry Hudson ordered the anchor to be lifted and the ship to be turned into the broad waterway. Hudson and his men were delighted with the beauty of the country which they passed as the *Half Moon* sailed up the river.

The mate's journal tells of many adventures. Usually the Indians were friendly and wanted to trade with the white men, but Hudson and his sailors were afraid of them. Once the Indians did attack the white men, and in the fight one sailor was killed. But the guns of the white men easily frightened the savages away.

A party of Indians paddled out in their canoes to see the strange ship

HENRY HUDSON 155

At the place that is now Catskill Landing, the Indians were very friendly. Henry Hudson consented to go ashore with some of them. They led him to the bark tepee of their Indian chief, where

The Indians, by breaking the arrows, showed that they wanted to be friendly

a feast had been prepared. In the meantime, other men of the tribe took presents of grapes, pumpkins, furs, and tobacco on board the *Half Moon*.

When the feast was over, Hudson started to go. But the Indians made signs inviting him to stay with them until morning. Hudson did not care to trust himself even with this friendly tribe, and the Indians were greatly disappointed. At last one of the men picked up a few arrows, broke them in pieces, and threw them on the fire. Now Hudson was sure that the Indians really wanted to be friends, but he did not stay overnight.

The *Half Moon* sailed as far up the river as the place where Albany, New York, now stands. Each day grew more and more disappointing. At last the water was so shallow that the ship could go no farther. A small boat was sent to explore, but it soon returned, and the brave Hudson had to give up all hope for success on this voyage. The passage had turned out to be a river. The Northwest Passage must be much farther along the coast to the north.

In the name of the Dutch merchants who had sent him on the voyage, Hudson took possession of the country he had explored. Then he sailed down the river, through the beautiful harbor, and across the Atlantic Ocean to the Old World. When the small ship came in sight of England, Hudson could not sail past his own home after being away so long and enduring so many dangers. So the *Half Moon* anchored in an English port.

Hudson sent a written report of the voyage to the Dutch East India Company. He told them of the beauty and richness of the new land that he had claimed for them. He asked for more money and

HENRY HUDSON

men to prepare for another trip in search of the Northwest Passage.

In answer to this report the Dutch merchants sent for Hudson to come to Holland. They wanted to talk the matter over carefully before sending him out again. But King James of England would not let him sail for any country but his own. The king said, "You are an Englishman. If any more exploring trips are made, they must be made for your own country. Besides, the land which you have claimed for the Dutch already belongs to England. John Cabot sailed along that coast and took possession of that land more than one hundred years ago." So Henry Hudson did not see the Dutch merchants again.

The Last Voyage

Everywhere, the men who were interested in exploration heard of the voyage of Henry Hudson. Again a group of Englishmen hired him to sail for them in search of a passage to India. Soon a little ship named the *Discovery* was ready for his use. In April, 1610, Hudson left England on his fourth voyage in search of a route to India.

This time he steered northwest across the Atlantic and reached the barren coast of Labrador. Sailing northward, he found an open waterway leading to the west. Eagerly he followed this passage and came into a great open sea. At last he had been successful, thought Hudson. This must be a great arm of the Pacific Ocean!

His crew wanted to return to England and report that the Northwest Passage had been found. But Hudson knew that he must prove that he was right before he could claim success. Eagerly he followed the southern shore of the open sea and pushed on in spite of the threats and complaints of his men. One day the small party of men who went ashore found in an Eskimo's storehouse a large enough supply of wild fowl to last all winter. But Hudson would not allow his men to stop for them. "Any day," he said, "the ship may be frozen in. Even a few hour's delay now might prevent us from reaching the open Pacific."

Sure enough, very soon the *Discovery* was frozen hard and fast in the ice of the great Hudson Bay.

Hudson, like Magellan and Drake, was a brave and fearless sailor. But the sailors with him were not so brave as their great leader. Sickness, hunger, and cold brought suffering to the men on the little *Discovery*. Sometimes for weeks they could find no game and had nothing but Arctic moss to eat. They came very near to starving during the long months of that terrible winter. It was June of the next year before the ice broke and the *Discovery* could sail through open water.

Hudson still felt sure that success lay just ahead, and he gave the order to raise the sails and turn toward the west.

The men were discouraged, and weak from the long winter of suffering. They decided that they could not sail any farther west, come what might, and they would take their ship home to England. Henry Hudson should no longer be their captain.

Into an open boat without provisions they put Hudson and his son John, who always sailed with him. In the same boat they also placed the sick men and those sailors who were faithful to the great explorer. Then they set the boat adrift from the *Discovery* and sailed for home.

A few of the rebellious sailors lived to reach home, but no one knows what happened to the small drifting boat of abandoned men. Henry Hudson

Hudson and his son and some sailors were set adrift in an open boat

THE NORTHWEST PASSAGE

and his companions were lost in the ice and snow of the great unknown North. They were never seen nor heard of again.

Here in America we speak the name "Hudson" too often ever to forget the brave English seaman whose life was lost in the cause of discovery. The great Hudson River which he explored was named for him. Far to the north, the great bay where he was lost and the strait which connects that bay with the Atlantic Ocean both bear his name.

HOW CAREFULLY DID YOU READ?

After reading the entire story, see if you can answer the questions. If you succeed, you have remembered the most important parts of the story.

1. For whom and where did Henry Hudson sail on his first two voyages of exploration?
2. Why did the Dutch East India Company want to find a shorter route to the East Indies?
3. Where did Henry Hudson sail for the Holland merchants and what did he find?
4. When Henry Hudson sailed on his last voyage, where did he go?
5. What places are named in honor of Henry Hudson?

Now take one question at a time, and read aloud the part of the story to prove your answer.

Trace on an outline map of the world:

1. Henry Hudson's first voyage north along the eastern coast of Greenland
2. His second voyage around the northern part of Norway
3. His third voyage to the coast of Maine and the Hudson River
4. His fourth voyage to the Hudson Bay

THE SETTLEMENT OF NEW YORK
PETER STUYVESANT
The Dutch Settle on Manhattan Island

Can you imagine a man in our time trying to buy Manhattan Island? It is no larger than some of our great western ranches, but part of the city of New York is built on this island. Great skyscrapers tower above the city streets, and subways carry crowds of busy workers under the ground. The land is so valuable that Manhattan could not be bought for thousands of millions of dollars. Yet a little more than three hundred years ago, the Dutch bought the entire island from the Indians for twenty-four dollars' worth of knives, beads, ribbons, and red cloth. And the Indians were well pleased with their bargain.

Not long after Henry Hudson's exploring trips to the New World, a few Dutch settlers and fur traders came to America. They took possession of the land near the Hudson River and called the place New Netherland. For a number of years Dutch merchants carried on a rich fur trade with the Indians of New Netherland. But the Dutch colony did not really begin to grow until Peter Minuit came as governor and made his famous bargain for Manhattan Island. That was seventeen years after

THE SETTLEMENT OF NEW YORK

Henry Hudson had sailed up the beautiful river and claimed the land around it for the Dutch.

More settlers came to New Netherland. Dutch houses appeared in little villages along the Hudson River, and on the islands in the harbor. Windmills like those in Holland were built, and their great arms could be seen turning when the winds blew. The farms grew larger, and the little settlement on Manhattan Island became the town of New Amsterdam, now New York City.

But the people were not always peaceful and happy. Sometimes they quarreled with the Indians and cheated them in trading for their furs. Then the Indians swooped down on a settlement, burned the houses, and killed the people. New governors came from the mother country, but they did not know how to deal with the Indians. They did not always rule the settlers wisely. Once the colonists sent a petition to Amsterdam to have the governor recalled.

Stuyvesant Becomes Governor

Finally the West India Company, which owned the American land, decided to send a new governor to the dissatisfied colonists. Peter Stuyvesant should go. They felt sure that he would rule well, for he had been a successful governor in another Dutch colony. He had been a good soldier, too, and would know how to protect the settlers.

The ship bringing Peter Stuyvesant to New Netherland anchored in the harbor of New Amsterdam

PETER STUYVESANT 163

one day in May, 1647. Many of the colonists were gathered to greet the new governor. When he came ashore, they saw a sturdy, proud old soldier, wearing an ostrich plume in his hat, and stamping along on a wooden leg. "One-legged Peter," and "Old Silver Leg," the colonists nicknamed him.

The colonists gathered to greet their new governor

Later, when they learned how hot-tempered was their honest old governor, they called him "Peter the Testy," and "Peter the Headstrong."

"I shall rule over you as a father rules his children," Governor Stuyvesant told the colonists. A good father, but a very stern one, was Peter Stuyvesant. He always had the good of the people at heart, and he did much to improve conditions in

THE SETTLEMENT OF NEW YORK

the colony. But he would not let the people help in the government. He himself made the laws, saw that they were obeyed, and tried and punished anyone who broke them. When the colonists threatened to send an appeal to the mother country, the hot-tempered governor replied, "If anyone appeals, I will make him a foot shorter and send the pieces to Holland and let him appeal in that way."

After many disputes, Governor Stuyvesant finally allowed the colonists to elect a council of nine men who were to help make the laws. But the council had very little power. Whenever it suggested something that agreed with the governor's ideas, the governor made it a law. If he did not agree, Peter the Testy flew into a rage, stamped on the floor with his wooden leg, and refused to allow the idea to be carried out.

The governor kept order among the settlers and controlled the Indians. He settled boundary disputes between New Netherland and her neighbors in New England. With money that he raised by taxing the merchants and traders he improved the town of New Amsterdam. He had the old fort torn down and a new one built of stone, with twenty cannon mounted and ready to defend the settle-

PETER STUYVESANT

ment. New Amsterdam was surrounded by water on three sides. To protect the little town on the land side, the governor built a strong wall of pointed logs. Peter Stuyvesant's wall extended across the island, where the modern Wall Street now cuts its way through the crowded business section of New York City.

The colony grew and prospered under Peter Stuyvesant's rule. New Amsterdam became a town of fifteen hundred people, while all the colonists living in the New Netherland settlements numbered ten thousand.

Dutch and English Claims to New Netherland

Each year England was growing more jealous of the Dutch colony that was planted on land that John Cabot had discovered and claimed for England so many years before. England wanted this fertile land with its splendid harbor. Besides, she did not want any other nation to hold land which lay between her colony of Virginia and her settlements in New England.

Governor Stuyvesant was on his guard against the English. He felt sure that some day he would need every defense which he could build to protect his colonists. He sent a message to Holland asking for soldiers. He wanted a small trained army to be stationed in his fort and brave seamen to help defend the coast. But help was delayed too long.

THE SETTLEMENT OF NEW YORK

One day in August, 1664, four English ships loaded with soldiers appeared in the harbor of New Amsterdam. Colonel Richard Nicolls, the commander of the fleet, sent a note to Governor Stuyvesant demanding the surrender of the town. Stuyvesant knew that the town, with its few soldiers and old cannon, could not hope to defend itself long against the large force of English. Yet he could not bring himself to yield without a fight. "While I have a leg to stand on and an arm to fight with, I will never surrender," he said.

Colonel Nicolls sent a second message — "If you surrender peacefully, not a man shall be hurt and no property shall be destroyed." Still Peter Stuyvesant refused to give up the town. When the council advised that the message should be read to the people, he tore the letter to pieces.

Some of the council rescued the scraps, patched them together, and read the message to the people. No one would support the governor in his stand against the English.

"We cannot hope to defeat them," said the colonists. "Besides, we have had no liberty under Governor Stuyvesant. English rule could not be worse. Let us surrender."

The Dutch governor could not fight the whole English army single-handed. He had to give up. The doors of the fort were opened, the English marched in, and their flag was raised where the Dutch colors had waved for more than half a century.

"New Amsterdam" became "New York" in honor of the Duke of York, the new owner of the colony. Soon all the territory of New Netherland surrendered to the English and became known as New York.

And what happened to Peter Stuyvesant? The honest old soldier returned to Europe and reported to the Dutch West India Company that the colony had surrendered. Then he came back to New York and spent the rest of his life at his comfortable farmhouse or "bowerie," as it was called. A part of New York City was afterward called the Bowery in memory of this house.

Like all Dutch homesteads, the "bowerie" was surrounded by a well-kept garden. Its neat flower

The message from the English was read to the people

168 THE SETTLEMENT OF NEW YORK

On summer evenings two friends might often have been seen walking in this garden

beds, shaped in circles, squares, and diamonds, bloomed with old-fashioned flowers. On pleasant summer evenings two friends might often have been seen walking in this garden. They enjoyed the flowers, the soft breeze, their pipes, and their friendly talk. I know you will be surprised, but you will also be glad, to know that these two friends were the English governor, Colonel Nicolls, and Peter Stuyvesant.

MAKING A SUMMARY

A summary is a short way of saying something. A good summary tells the most important part of a longer statement. This longer statement may be a paragraph, a part of a selection, or a whole story. When your teacher calls on you to recite, she really expects you to give a summary of a part of a lesson.

Here is a summary for the topic, **The Dutch Settle Manhattan Island**: The Dutch paid the Indians twenty-four dollars for Manhattan Island, now part of the immensely

PETER STUYVESANT

valuable city of New York. They built up the fur trade and cleared farms. Their unfair treatment of the Indians caused Indian wars.

Now write a summary for one of the other headings in this chapter.

Locate on a map:

    Manhattan Island   Albany

THE FRENCH IN CANADA

Samuel de Champlain

Early Life in France

On the eastern coast of France is the quiet little village of Brouage. Three hundred fifty years ago, Brouage was a busy city. Schooners and fishing boats sailed from its harbor, and warships of France anchored there. That was when Samuel de Champlain was a boy and played on its wharves.

Samuel's father was a sea captain who taught his son how to steer a boat and manage the sails in any kind of weather. Samuel loved the sea, and he became a good sailor. But when he grew up, he did not stay in Brouage. A war broke out in France, and young Champlain joined the army. For more than ten years he was a soldier, fighting and marching in France.

Champlain Learns About America

At last the war ended and Champlain was free. He went to Spain. There he was given a chance to do something he liked much better than fighting. A Spanish fleet was sailing for America, and Champlain was put in command of one of the ships.

SAMUEL DE CHAMPLAIN

The fleet visited most of the important seaports of the West Indies and Mexico. Champlain learned much about the life in Spanish America. He made maps of the places he visited, and he drew pictures of the strange animals he saw. He made several trips into the interior and found out as much as he could about this new country and the Indians who lived there.

When Champlain finally returned to France, he sent to the king an enthusiastic report of his travels in the New World. The king and many of the nobles were much interested in the report, for France also claimed a large part of America. They hoped that some day New France might become as rich a colony as New Spain, with towns, cattle, and fertile fields. This French land lay far to the north of Mexico, where Canada now is.

More than sixty years had passed since the Frenchman, Cartier, had explored the region about the St. Lawrence River and claimed it for France. During those sixty years, very little had been learned about this new land. Every year the hardy French fishermen visited its coasts, but they knew nothing about the country except near the coast. A few merchants had begun to carry on a fur trade with the Indians. A few settlements had been started and had failed. New France was still as Cartier had found it, a land of the Indian and the wild animal.

One of the French noblemen who heard Champlain's report wished to start a settlement in America.

He decided to learn more about the country before sending colonists. Who could be better equipped than Champlain to explore the land and bring back a complete description of what he had seen? The king approved the plan, and Champlain was eager to go. Thus it happened that in 1603, two small ships sailed into the Gulf of St. Lawrence bringing Champlain to New France for the first time.

Many times afterward, Champlain made the trip between France and America. But he never forgot what he saw on this first arrival. He marveled at the size of the St. Lawrence River, and at the beautiful forests that covered its banks. In a small boat he sailed far up the river to the rapids which Cartier had named La Chine because he thought they blocked the way to China. Champlain and a few friendly Indian guides tried to go up the rapids in their small boat, but they had to give up and turn back to the quiet water below.

The Indians tried to make the white men understand what they would find above the rapids. When words and signs failed, the red men drew on the deck a picture of a large body of water and a tumbling waterfall. As clearly as they could, the Indian artists showed Niagara Falls and Lake Ontario.

When Champlain returned to France, he gave a glowing account of the beautiful country which he had seen and of the rich furs that could be bought from the Indian hunters. A few years later, in

1608, he himself was leading a little colony back to settle on the banks of the St. Lawrence.

Champlain Plants a Colony at Quebec

Champlain followed the St. Lawrence River far into the country, past a large island which divided the river into two narrow streams. At last, on the northern shore of the river, he saw the steep rocks of a high cliff. On his first trip he had chosen this place, and there Quebec, the oldest city in Canada, was built. A fort on that rocky cliff would be a strong defense against an army of English or Spanish soldiers, or an attack of savage Indians.

Champlain, however, had already made friends with the surrounding Indians and had no fear of attack by them. The first cabins were built on the bank of the river below the cliff, not far from the present market place of the Lower Town of Quebec. The present streets of this quaint old city follow the winding trails of the forest where Champlain and his men often walked.

In numbers, this French settlement was smaller than either Jamestown or Plymouth, but the experiences of the settlers were much the same. There were only twenty-eight men in the small town of Quebec, twenty-eight men who did not know how to prepare for the bitter cold of a Canadian winter. There was much suffering and sickness, and many died. In May, when a French ship arrived with more colonists and supplies, only seven men besides Champlain were left in the colony, and most of these were weak and ill.

Champlain and the Indians

The winter had been a hard one for the Indians as well as for the white men. When game became so scarce that the red men were hungry, the kind-hearted governor shared his own food with the Indians. The Indians were very grateful. They grew to love Champlain and became great friends of the French settlers.

When the long winter was over, the Indians gathered a great war party to go against their enemies, the Iroquois. Would not their brother Champlain go with them and help them to win the battle? Champlain wanted to show the Indians that he was really their friend. Besides, he thought that this trip would give him a fine chance to explore the country. Perhaps the northwest passage to China could be found in the country of the Iroquois. So he and a few of his soldiers went with the Indians.

The Iroquois lived in what is now the state of New York. Champlain's Indian friends, the Algonquins and the Hurons, must travel southward for many days before they could reach the Iroquois country. They turned from the St. Lawrence into a smaller stream and paddled southward day after day.

At last they came to the long, beautiful body of water which is now called after the explorer, Lake Champlain. This was Iroquois country and the

Champlain and the Algonquins boldly attacked the Iroquois

Algonquins went forward cautiously. They traveled only at night, and they hid their canoes as soon as the gray morning light appeared.

One night the Indians in the first canoe saw moving objects ahead of them. In a few minutes the terrible war whoop of the Iroquois sounded on the still night air. The Algonquins answered and a great chase began, for the Iroquois did not want to be caught on the lake. They succeeded in reaching the shore and escaping into the forest. Quickly the Iroquois cut down trees and piled them up to make a rude fort.

In the morning the Algonquins attacked. The Iroquois did not stay in their fort, but came boldly out to meet their enemies. Champlain and his men, dressed in armor and wearing plumed helmets, stepped out in front of the Algonquins and raised their muskets.

The Iroquois had never seen white men before, and did not fear the muskets. With a yell, their brave chiefs rushed forward just as the guns of the white men spoke. Several of the Indians fell, among them the two chiefs. At the same moment Algonquin arrows flew thick and fast. But the terrible "fire sticks" of the white men had already done their work. The Iroquois warriors all turned and ran into the forest, leaving their canoes, and a large supply of weapons behind. It was a great victory for the northern Indians. When they returned home, the Algonquins celebrated the triumph by a great feast and war dance.

This battle was most unfortunate for the French. The powerful Iroquois Indians never forgave them for helping the Algonquins. Many years later, when war broke out between the French and the English settlers, the Iroquois Indians fought with the English and helped to destroy French power in America.

SAMUEL DE CHAMPLAIN

Champlain's Life in Canada

During the years that Champlain spent in America, he made many exploring trips and founded many fur-trading stations. On one of these trips he traveled up the St. Lawrence River to Mount Royal, below the La Chine rapids. Here he started the settlement which became the great city of Montreal. On another trip he traveled far up the Ottawa River. After a short journey overland, he came to a great inland sea many times the size of Lake Champlain. This was Lake Huron. With his Indian friends, Champlain paddled across the lake. Then he traveled overland to the eastern end of Lake Ontario and crossed into the present state of New York.

Champlain thought that the French traders and settlers should learn the Indian language and understand how the Indians lived. He sent several of his men to live for a while with Indian tribes, and he himself spent one winter among the Hurons. Later on, he brought missionaries from France to teach the Indians the white men's religion and ways of living.

The Indians knew that Champlain, the great white governor whom they loved, was always just and fair with them. They came to feel that they could trust their French friends, and in turn were friendly and helpful to the French.

Champlain's methods of dealing with the Indians were learned and used by all the French fur traders

178   THE FRENCH IN CANADA

who came to America. As a result, the French never had the trouble with the Indians that the Spanish and English settlers had. The Spanish made slaves of the Indians and compelled them to work on the land which once the red men had owned. The English were friendly only when they

The French fur traders were always received kindly by the Indians

wanted something from the Indians, but they always distrusted the red men and treated them as savages. Naturally, the Indians liked the French the best.

The fur traders and trappers of New France could go safely among the Indians. Far into the interior of Canada, where the animals with the best furs could be found, went these traders. *Coureurs de bois*, forest rangers, men called them. They wore leggings,

SAMUEL DE CHAMPLAIN

moccasins, and deer-skin jackets like those worn by the Indians. Often they lived for months in an Indian village, sharing the red man's food and wigwam. Many Frenchmen learned to enjoy this life of adventure in the great Canadian wilderness. Many a French boy in the settlements of New France longed for the day when he could be a trapper and travel into the great forests of the North and West.

The fur trade was very profitable and brought wealth to the traders and to France. Slowly the French settlements grew. Farms and villages appeared where once Champlain had seen only forests and Indian trails.

For thirty years Champlain was governor of New France and worked for the good of the colonists. So much did he do for this new land which he loved, that even today men call him "the Father of New France."

COMPLETING AN OUTLINE

Fill in the blanks in the following outline:

I. Early Life in France.

II. Champlain Learns About America
    1. Champlain's trip with the Spanish fleet
    2. Early French claims
    3. ----------------------------------

III. Champlain Plants a Colony at Quebec
    1. ----------------------------------
    2. ----------------------------------

THE FRENCH IN CANADA

IV. Champlain and the Indians
    1. Making friends with the Indians
    2. ....

V. Champlain's Life in Canada
    1. ....
    2. ....

Find on the map in your geography:

France	Hudson River
Montreal	Great Lakes
Quebec	St. Lawrence River
Lake Champlain	Appalachian Mountain Range

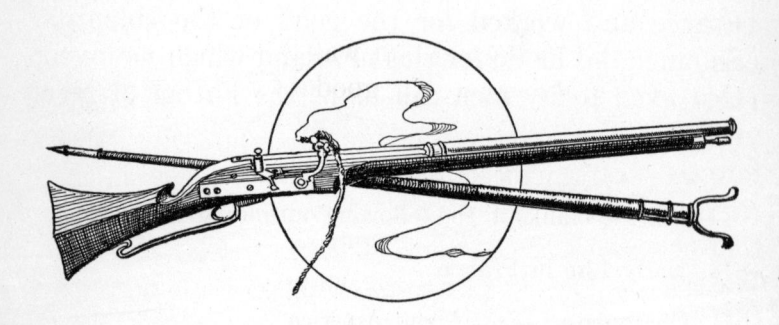

DOWN THE MISSISSIPPI
Robert La Salle
Searching for the Mississippi River

The Spaniards did not know how mighty was the great river that Ferdinand De Soto had discovered during his search for gold in 1541. They did not know that half a continent poured its streams into the muddy Mississippi. They did not even guess how vast and rich was the Mississippi Valley, with its thousands of miles of forests and prairies. They made no effort to explore the river any farther than De Soto's men had gone. For a hundred years its existence was almost forgotten.

Little by little the French traders from the settlements which Champlain had founded pushed farther into the western wilderness. As they traveled in the region of the Great Lakes, they met Indians who told them of a great western river, the "Father of Waters." The Frenchmen thought that perhaps this great river flowed into the Pacific Ocean. Perhaps it was the long-sought-for passage to China! They questioned the Indians eagerly.

"Where is the great river?"

The red men pointed to the setting sun.

"How far?"

"Many days' journey."

Day after day Marquette and Joliet followed the course of the Mississippi

"Does it empty into the great western ocean?"

The Indians did not know. But the tales of the mysterious river made the French eager to learn more about its course. Finally, in 1673, a small party of men was sent out by Frontenac, who was then governor of New France. Led by Joliet, a fur trader, and Marquette, a missionary, the little band started to find and to explore the Mississippi River.

From the familiar waters of Lake Huron, the men and their Indian guides traveled in birch-bark canoes into the less known Lake Michigan. Along the northern shore they paddled, into Green Bay and up the Fox River. From the Fox River, a short trail through the forest, called a *portage*, led to the Wisconsin River. Across this portage the explorers and their Indian guides carried the canoes and supplies. Then they launched their little fleet on the Wisconsin River, and followed the winding stream until they reached the Mississippi.

Day after day the party followed the course of the Mississippi River southward. Day after day they watched for a turn to the west. Often the river curved in that direction, only to turn south once more. As far as the mouth of the Arkansas River, went Marquette and Joliet. They were sure now that the river did not lead to the western ocean. They decided to turn back to Canada.

When the French explorers returned, they told of the rich and beautiful country they had seen. They declared that the Mississippi River did not lead to the Pacific Ocean, but probably flowed into the Gulf of Mexico.

Robert La Salle

Among those who heard the story of Marquette and Joliet was Robert La Salle, a young Frenchman who had come to Canada to make his fortune. After a few years, he was put in command of a new fort, called Fort Frontenac, at the eastern end of Lake Ontario. The fort became an important center of trade, and many Indians settled close by for protection from their Iroquois enemies. Trappers and missionaries came to the fort for supplies. Here they said farewell to the white man's world when they plunged into the western wilderness.

La Salle was much interested in the wild and lonely land that surrounded the tiny settlements and made several exploring trips. On one of these trips he had discovered the Ohio River and claimed all the land around it for France.

La Salle began to grow rich at Fort Frontenac, but wealth did not interest him. He kept thinking of other exploring trips which he wanted to make. When he heard about the journey of Marquette and Joliet, he knew that he would never be satisfied until he could follow the Mississippi to its mouth and win for France the land through which it flowed. France should have a great water highway through America. From the mouth of the St. Lawrence on the shores of the Atlantic, it would lead by way of the Great Lakes, to the Gulf of Mexico where the Mississippi flowed into the sea. He would build forts along the Mississippi like those along the St. Lawrence. These forts would secure the fur trade and protect the French land from other countries that might try to claim it.

ROBERT LA SALLE

La Salle made a special trip to France to win the king's permission to carry out his exploring plans. With the king's consent, he brought back to Canada all the supplies he might need, and men to go with him on the long journey. Among these men was an Italian who became his most faithful friend — Henry Tonty.

The exploring party reached Fort Frontenac in the autumn of 1678. At once the men started to carry out La Salle's plans. The explorer had decided to build a sailing ship for the long journey by water. Since he knew that no ship could sail past the falls of Niagara, he sent Tonty with the shipbuilding crew above the falls to a place on the Niagara River near Lake Erie. There, during the long, cold winter, the men worked on the boat. At last it was finished. On the prow was carved a great monster called a *griffin*, and *Griffin* the boat was named.

August of 1679 had come before the little expedition was ready to start. Loaded with men and supplies, the *Griffin* began the long journey westward. As the wind filled her sails, the Indians looked on in wonder. They were watching the first "white-winged boat" ever to sail on Lake Erie.

The *Griffin* sailed from Lake Erie up the Detroit River to Lake Huron. Several times the party stopped to trade for furs. At last they reached the Strait of Mackinac, which connects Lake Huron with Lake Michigan. After they had again collected furs, the *Griffin* was loaded with such a rich cargo that La Salle decided to send the boat back to Fort Frontenac. The furs would sell for enough to pay most of the expenses of the expedition, and the captain could return at once with more supplies for the voyagers.

The men did not like to give up their comfortable quarters in the boat, and they grumbled a great deal about the change of plan. But the *Griffin* started back, and La Salle bargained with the Indians for canoes in which to continue the journey. Soon the party was traveling southward along the shore of Lake Michigan. When they reached the mouth of the St. Joseph River, the men landed and built a fort while they waited for the *Griffin*.

But the ship did not return. Weeks went by and winter came with no news of the white-sailed ship. The *Griffin* had disappeared. Two men were sent to Mackinac to watch for its return, but La Salle never learned whether his boat had been lost in a storm or destroyed by savages. No one ever again heard of the *Griffin*. For many months La Salle would not give up hope for his ship, but he decided to go on without it. The explorers would have to eat, sleep, and travel just as the Indians did, but La Salle would not give up his plan of exploring the Mississippi to its mouth.

La Salle Meets Many Difficulties

The travelers journeyed up the St. Joseph River until they came to an Indian trail through the woods which led to the Illinois River. Following their Indian guides, the little party carried their canoes through the forest. They waded through ice and snow and crossed frozen swamps, but finally they found a small stream which led them to the Illinois River which flows westward into the Mississippi.

The way was now easy to find, but the journey was dangerous. The Indians of this region belonged to the Illinois tribe and were friendly to the French. But the Iroquois, those old enemies of the French, were at war with these western Indians. At any moment the white men might meet a party of Iroquois warriors. Sometimes the explorers did not dare to shoot game or even to build a camp fire for fear of being discovered. They were often cold and hungry.

Cautiously they followed the Illinois River until it widened into a lake, now called Lake Peoria. Where the river again narrowed, La Salle discovered a large Indian camp with tepees on both sides of the river. Would these savages prove to be friends or foes? They had already seen the white men, and La Salle ordered all his canoes to advance side by side. As they drew near the village, each man was ready to drop his paddle and seize a gun. Soon, however, the Indians who were watching on the shore made signs of friendship and the Frenchmen knew that they belonged to the Illinois tribe.

La Salle and his men landed and were treated as honored guests. After the peace pipe had been smoked and a feast eaten, La Salle spoke to the warriors of the village. He said, "We have come as friends and wish to build a fort which will help to protect you from your enemies. We also want to build a large wooden canoe in which to sail down the great 'Father of Waters.' If you will help us and give us food, we will live together as brothers and will supply you with the white man's guns so that you can conquer your enemies."

The Indians seemed much pleased and promised to help their new friends. But during the night an Indian scout stole into camp and brought a false report that La Salle was an Iroquois spy. The old chief believed the story and thought that La Salle wished to go down the Mississippi in order to persuade the southern Indians to join in the war against the Illinois.

In the morning the chief called another council and warned La Salle against exploring the Mississippi. The river, he said, was full of rocks, terrible monsters would devour the men, or whirlpools would swallow up the boat.

Fortunately La Salle understood the reason for this change, for a friendly young warrior had already told him what had happened. La Salle answered the old chief boldly, saying that he had no fear of monsters and whirlpools and understood the reason for these warnings. Some of the Frenchmen, however were not so fearless. That night six of them ran away, and one of the others made an unsuccessful attempt to poison their leader.

ROBERT LA SALLE

The explorers left the Indian camp and journeyed a short distance down the Illinois River, where they found a suitable place and built a fort. Here, too, they began to build a sailing vessel for the long trip down the Mississippi River. Tonty was left in charge of the men while La Salle with five companions returned to Fort Frontenac. It was a long, dangerous journey, but they must have an anchor, ropes, and sails for the boat, supplies for the men, and articles of trade for the Indians. In spite of the delay and hardships, La Salle felt that the trip back was necessary.

This journey of about one thousand miles to Fort Frontenac was made in a little over two months. It was probably the hardest trip ever undertaken by a French explorer. Thick forests grew south of the Great Lakes, and through these La Salle and his men traveled on foot. The spring rains came down in floods and there was constant danger from wild animals and from the savage Iroquois Indians. When the small party reached the western end of Lake Erie, they built a canoe and traveled by water, carrying the boat on their shoulders around the great Niagara Falls.

La Salle's strength helped him to withstand the hardships. This was fortunate, for troubles now came thick and fast. The last hope for the *Griffin* was gone and all the valuable furs which she carried were lost. A trapper from the western wilderness brought a letter from Tonty saying that most of the men had deserted soon after La Salle left. They had taken what they wanted from the supplies and had gone to trade for themselves and to live with the Indians. Finally a ship bringing supplies from France had been wrecked at the mouth of the St. Lawrence River. This meant a great loss, and it also meant that La Salle must travel as far as Montreal in order to buy the things that he needed.

In spite of all these troubles, La Salle did not give up his plans. Three months after he arrived at Frontenac, he was ready to return to the help of the faithful Tonty and his few remaining men. With him went twenty-five new explorers to share his fortunes in the West.

Again La Salle came to the Illinois River. On the way down the river, his men noticed signs of Indian warfare. The village where La Salle had asked for help was burned to the ground. This must have been the work of the Iroquois, who had attacked the friendly Illinois tribes and driven them from their homes.

The Frenchmen pushed on as fast as possible. What would they find at their own fort? There was the hill where it had been built, but the place was deserted and the fort in ruins. The partly finished sailboat was found, but every nail and piece of metal had been taken. A plank was also found on which was written in French, "We are all savages." This was probably the message left by the deserters of whom Tonty wrote. But where was

ROBERT LA SALLE

Tonty himself? La Salle knew that his faithful friend had stayed by the fort as long as he could defend it. Had he escaped or had he been taken prisoner or killed by the Iroquois?

During that winter La Salle searched for Tonty and encouraged the Illinois Indians to come back to their hunting grounds and to unite with him against their enemies. He promised that the French would send guns in trade for furs. This time the Illinois Indians believed him and became strong friends of the French.

In every Indian camp, La Salle asked for news of his faithful friend. At last he found that Tonty and four Frenchmen had escaped from the Iroquois and started north in a canoe. It was welcome news, and proved to be true; for Tonty was found safe and well in a French fort on the shore of Lake Michigan.

The two friends had many adventures to tell each other when they met. But as soon as the stories were told, they began to plan for their much delayed journey down the Mississippi.

Twice Robert La Salle had prepared for this exploring trip, and twice he had met failure. But once more he and his friends returned to Canada to get the needed help and supplies.

For this third expedition La Salle did not try to build a sailboat, but decided to use canoes well loaded with supplies. The party was now larger than at first. There were twenty-three French explorers, eighteen faithful Indian guides, ten squaws to do the cooking, and three children whom the Indian women would not leave behind.

Down the Mississippi

Another winter had come before they were ready to start. But La Salle was eager for the journey and would not wait for spring. Sleds were made, and the canoes and supplies were hauled over the ice and snow. In spite of the cold weather, the brave La Salle and his followers pushed on. When they reached the lower part of the Illinois River, the ice had broken. They launched the canoes and the whole party paddled into the Mississippi, the great Father of Waters.

Floating ice delayed the travelers for a time, but they soon passed into open water and reached the place where the city of St. Louis now stands. Here the Missouri River flows into the Mississippi. Farther and farther south the party journeyed. The weather became warmer, and wild cotton was seen growing along the banks of the river.

In one place they found an Indian village with small huts made of sun-baked mud mixed with straw. These were the first Indian houses the French had ever seen built in this way. They were surprised to find that all Indians did not live in tepees made of skins or bark.

The journey down the river was slow, for La Salle stopped to build forts along the way. At last the

ROBERT LA SALLE 193

La Salle claimed the land in the name of King Louis of France

party reached the place where the great Mississippi River divides into three broad streams. Some of the canoes followed each of these streams, and soon they reached the Gulf of Mexico.

On April 9, 1682, the party met a short distance above the mouth of the river. La Salle planted a tall post on which was written in French "Louis the Great, King of France, rules here." Then he declared that all the land along the Ohio and Mississippi rivers and along all their branches belonged to King Louis of France. He named that great tract of land *Louisiana*, "Louis's land." As the French flag waved for the first time at the mouth of the Mississippi River, the explorers sang with joy, fired their guns, and shouted "Long live the king." He had found the mouth of the Mississippi River and had given to France a wonderful new territory many times as large as the present state of Louisiana.

After four years of hardship and disappointment, La Salle had at last met with success. On the return trip, the explorers remained in the Illinois country to continue their work of making friends with the Indians. Not far from the spot where they had built their first forts they chose a high rocky cliff, now called Starved Rock. Here they built another fort which they named Fort St. Louis. Indians of many tribes settled near by, and Tonty was left in command of the fort.

La Salle returned to Quebec, and then sailed to France to report his success to the king. La Salle had already formed a new plan and he had a favor to ask of His Majesty as well as a report to make. He asked King Louis of France to give him ships and men so that he might build a fort and settlement at the mouth of the Mississippi River. This fort would help to hold and defend the land for France. The king was willing to grant this request, and soon four ships with about two hundred eighty

ROBERT LA SALLE

men were sailing from France toward the Gulf of Mexico.

Lost but Not Discouraged

This expedition met with nothing but misfortune. One ship was captured by the Spaniards, the others went too far west, and La Salle was unable to find the mouth of the Mississippi River. At last the men landed on the coast of Texas and built a fort.

The soldiers and settlers were growing discontented. They were angry with La Salle for losing the way. The largest ship sailed back to France and the two remaining ones were wrecked while exploring the coast in search of the mouth of the Mississippi River.

Many of the company became sick. All were unhappy and suffering from the poor water and the lack of food. Finally the men refused longer to obey the commands of La Salle. Still the brave leader was not willing to give up. He decided to take a few men, make the long journey by land to Tonty at Fort St. Louis, and bring help for those left behind. Just as he was about to set out on this long, hard trip, one of his own men hidden in the woods, shot and killed the brave leader.

Left alone, with no one to guide them, the explorers were indeed helpless. A few finally reached Fort St. Louis, and the faithful Tonty started out to rescue the others. But the poor colonists could not be found. They had all died of disease, had been killed by the Indians, or had been captured by the Spanish. Tonty's own men deserted him, and he finally made his way back to the fort, where he remained in command for many years.

La Salle had failed to finish the great work which he started. But he had shown the French what a vast, rich country lay between the Great Lakes and the Gulf of Mexico. He had opened the Mississippi Valley to the trader and the settler, and had added thousands of square miles to New France.

Thirty years after the death of La Salle, a French town — New Orleans — was built just where La Salle had hoped to start his colony. From the Gulf of Mexico to the Gulf of St. Lawrence, the great water highway was complete.

FINDING YOUR WAY

You probably cannot remember all the details of La Salle's journeys. Choose the important items from the following list:

1. La Salle became rich at Fort Frontenac.
2. La Salle planned to establish French claims to the Mississippi Valley.
3. The *Griffin* was lost.
4. The explorers traveled a thousand miles in two months.
5. La Salle kept on, in spite of many disasters, until he had followed the Mississippi River to its mouth and had claimed the Mississippi Valley for France.
6. La Salle was murdered by one of his own men.

Locate on a map in your geography:

Lake Ontario	Mackinac Island	Illinois River
Montreal, Canada	Green Bay	Missouri River
Niagara Falls	Wisconsin River	New Orleans

THE FRENCH AND INDIAN WAR
WOLFE AND MONTCALM
Rival Claims in the New World

The explorations of Champlain and La Salle had added a great deal of land to New France. Because of Champlain's explorations and the forts he had built, France claimed all the land on both sides of the St. Lawrence River. Because of La Salle's explorations and the forts he had built, France claimed all the land on both sides of the Mississippi River and the rivers flowing into the Mississippi.

All this land made New France much larger than the narrow strip of seacoast where the English colonists had made their homes. But still there were many more English than French settlements, and many more English than French in the New World. From the English strip of seacoast, the settlers were constantly pushing farther westward and making new settlements in the wilderness. In Virginia and Pennsylvania the settlements had reached the Appalachian Mountains. Here and there bold settlers were beginning to cross into the rich land that lay beyond the mountains, the land claimed by France.

Very soon the two nations were quarreling over the land that lay west of the Appalachian Mountains. The English would not accept the French claim, but said that the land belonged to the English colonies. Long before, the early settlers had received charters from England, giving them permission to settle certain parts of the Atlantic coast. Although the northern and southern boundaries of the colonies were clearly stated in these charters, the colonists could use the land to the westward as far as they wished. Their rights extended clear across the continent to the Pacific coast, which was thought to be much nearer the Atlantic than it really is. Besides, as a favor to some of the settlers of Virginia, the king had granted them large tracts of western land. The gifts of the king would be worthless if the French claims were accepted.

The Struggle for the Ohio River Valley

The French tried to strengthen their hold on the Ohio River country. They made friendly treaties with many of the Indian tribes. All along the Allegheny River and the upper part of the Ohio, they planted leaden plates claiming the land for France. They also began to build more forts.

News of what the French were doing alarmed some of the Virginians. Governor Dinwiddie decided to send a message to the French, warning them that they were using English land. If the French would not heed the message and leave willingly, he was determined to drive them out by force.

George Washington, a gallant young woodsman of Virginia, was chosen to carry the message to the

WOLFE AND MONTCALM

French. They replied politely, but paid no attention to the warning. Then colonial soldiers from Virginia were sent into the disputed land to build forts for the English. The first place chosen for a fort was in western Pennsylvania, where the Allegheny and the Monongahela rivers join to form the Ohio. Before the fort could be completed, the French attacked the Virginians, drove them out, finished the fort for themselves, and named it Fort Duquesne.

So the French and Indian War began. Across the Atlantic Ocean, France and England took up their colonists' quarrel, and sent soldiers to America to protect the land which they claimed in the New World. The fighting that started as a dispute over a few forts, grew into a struggle between two great nations to decide which should rule North America.

Most of the Indian tribes were friends of the French and helped them in the war. But the Iroquois Indians had never forgiven the French for helping their enemies many years before when Champlain first came to America. When trouble began, the Iroquois Indians and their allies fought on the English side. Because the Indians joined in the fighting, the English settlers called it the French and Indian War.

The French were brave soldiers and their Indian friends were cruel fighters. Many times small English towns were surprised in the night by bands

200   THE FRENCH AND INDIAN WAR

of Indians. The people were killed or taken prisoners, and their homes were burned. The English, too, and their friends the Iroquois, were very cruel. On both sides the war was frightful.

Troops were sent from England to help the English colonists, but the generals of the English army were not so skilful as the leaders of the French.

Many people were taken prisoners

For several years the English failed in every effort against the French.

The first great disaster was the attempt to recapture Fort Duquesne. General Braddock, with well-trained English soldiers, was sent to attack this important position and drive out the French. With Braddock went George Washington, now a young Virginian colonel.

The journey from Virginia into western Pennsylvania was a hard one. General Braddock had led his army on many a long march, but never through a wilderness like this. His progress was very slow, for he stopped to cut trees and build bridges so that his soldiers might march in orderly columns, and the baggage wagons might be brought along more easily.

Braddock formed his men in a solid line of battle

Long before the journey was over, Indian scouts were keeping the French at Fort Duquesne informed of the progress of the English soldiers.

At last General Braddock was only eight miles from Fort Duquesne. Suddenly from all sides came an attack. The French and Indians were hidden behind trees and bushes, and poured a terrific fire into the ranks of the English soldiers. Bullets sang and arrows flew in every direction. The Virginians sprang to cover and began fighting in this same Indian fashion, but Braddock formed his men in a solid line of battle and gave the order to fire. Again and again the command was obeyed, although the British could see no enemy at whom to aim. The red coats of their own uniforms were massed closely together and made an easy target for the French and Indians. The poor soldiers became terrified and confused. General Braddock did his best to keep control of his men, but they broke ranks and fled. Many were shot down before they could escape, and General Braddock was killed.

After this terrible English defeat, the French and their Indian allies grew bolder in their attacks on the frontier settlements. The English cause seemed almost hopeless.

William Pitt and Victory

At last William Pitt, the greatest statesman in England, was given the entire management of the war. He immediately sent new and better generals to lead the armies in America, and promised that England would furnish guns, ammunition, and supplies for any colonial soldiers who would fight for the mother country. Many brave colonists volunteered, and soon the fortunes of war changed.

In the summer of 1758, Louisburg, the French fort near the Gulf of St. Lawrence, was captured, and a few weeks later Fort Frontenac on Lake Ontario was destroyed. News that the English held possession of Lake Ontario and thus blocked the road to Canada, alarmed the French commander at Fort Duquesne. Some of the Indian allies deserted the French, and Fort Duquesne was soon captured by the English. Once more the fort became an English stronghold, and its name was changed to Fort Pitt in honor of William Pitt, the great Englishman. Today the city of Pittsburgh stands on the same spot where the struggles for Fort Duquesne took place.

Wolfe and Montcalm

The next year brought more success to England. Fort Niagara was captured, the last important French fort except Quebec. That city was well guarded by a strong force of French and Indians and commanded by a brave and skilful French general, Montcalm.

Young General Wolfe was chosen to lead the English forces against Quebec. In June, 1759, English warships carrying Wolfe and his army sailed up the St. Lawrence River to an island almost opposite Quebec. Across the river rose the rocky cliffs, at the top of which stood the frowning fort of the capital of New France. There seemed no way to reach the enemy, and General Wolfe's cannon could not batter down Nature's solid walls of stone. The cliff both above and below the fort was defended by cannon to keep the English from landing and making an attack from the rear.

THE FRENCH AND INDIAN WAR

General Montcalm felt safe, but he was a cautious soldier and kept a close guard. The summer passed. He thought that the English would soon be without food. And they certainly would have to sail away in the fall before their ships were frozen in the river. In the meantime, how could an army land in the face of the French guns? "We must not suppose," said General Montcalm, "that the enemy has wings."

All during the summer General Wolfe tried to find a way to attack the fort. Finally, early in September, he made a plan. A steep, rocky trail had been found leading straight up the cliff. With English warships in front of Quebec and an army at the top of the cliff, supplies could be cut off from the city, and Montcalm could be forced to fight.

On September 12, 1759, the night was dark, so dark that boats full of soldiers could not be seen. Once the moving boats were heard, and a French sentry called, "Who goes there?"

A Scotch officer who could speak French answered, "Provision boats. Don't make a noise. The English will hear you." The guard let them pass.

The English landed in a small bay which has since been named Wolfe's Cove. The twenty-four men who had volunteered to make the first ascent began to climb up the cliff on hands and knees, clinging to rocks and shrubs. On the shore waited the rest of the English soldiers. When the first men did not return, the boats were sent back for more of the army, and those on shore started up the trail.

WOLFE AND MONTCALM

At the top of the cliff behind the fort was a level field, called the Plains of Abraham. The first light of day showed an English army drawn up in splendid order on the plain. The French were completely surprised and quickly prepared for battle. The fighting did not last long. When the English charged with their bayonets. the French turned and ran.

Both generals were in the thick of the fighting and both were shot during the first firing. As General Wolfe was carried to the back of the battlefield, he heard shouts, "They run, they run!"

"Who run?" he asked.

"The French, Sir," was the answer.

"God be praised," said General Wolfe, "then I can die in peace."

When Montcalm was told that he could live only a few hours, he said, "Thank God, then I shall not live to see the surrender of Quebec."

The battle of Quebec was very important in the history of America. It gave the victory to the English in the French and Indian War. Montreal and the few remaining French forts soon surrendered. France was defeated, and when the treaty of peace was signed in 1763, she gave to England all of Canada and all the land east of the Mississippi River. North America, today, still feels the results of General Wolfe's great victory at Quebec, for the French and Indian War decided that this country should be an English nation and not a French one.

THE FRENCH AND INDIAN WAR

MAKING AN OUTLINE

An outline will help you to find and to remember the important points in any lesson. There are four main headings in this chapter. Copy them on your paper and number them I, II, III, IV.

Now write on your paper the important points under each of the headings; for example:

I. Rival Claims in the New World
    1. French claims
    2. English claims

II. The Struggle for the Ohio River Valley
    1. Washington's warning
    2. Building ....
    3. ....

Finish the outline of the chapter.

Find on a map in your geography:

Allegheny River	Ohio River	Quebec
Monongahela River		Pittsburgh, Pennsylvania

European settlements in eastern North America

ENGLAND AND HER COLONIES
AMERICAN PATRIOTS
Progress in the Thirteen English Colonies

More than one hundred fifty years had passed between 1607, when Captain John Smith came to Jamestown, and the close of the French and Indian War in 1763. During this century and a half, the English colonists had learned many things.

The first thing which they learned was that they must depend upon themselves and the wilderness in which they lived for their food. Supplies from England could not come often enough to feed all the settlers. Food had to be obtained by planting corn and other grains, by hunting game, and by fishing. The earliest colonists, therefore, became farmers, hunters, and fishermen.

In a few years, a family was able to raise more food than it needed. Then a carpenter or a miller could work at his own trade and exchange his labor for the food which his neighbors were raising. In this way all sorts of business were started.

Another lesson which the colonists learned was that different parts of the country were suited to different kinds of work. In New England, the fields were hard to plow because of the rocks and hills. But fine fish were caught in great numbers all along

AMERICAN PATRIOTS

the coast. The northern forests furnished splendid lumber, and the many short rivers gave good water power for running mills. The most successful colonists in New England learned to use these gifts of Nature, and became fishermen, shipbuilders, millers, and merchants.

In the southern colonies, the mountains were farther back from the seacoast. The fertile soil and mild climate made this the best part of the country for farming. Virginia farmers, or planters as they were called, became some of the most prosperous citizens of America. Great quantities of grain and tobacco were raised on their broad acres and shipped to England. In exchange, tools, harness, coaches, furniture, dishes, fine silks, and linens were brought back to be sold in America.

Almost three million people were now living on the narrow strip of land between the Appalachian Mountains and the Atlantic seacoast. Their land stretched from Maine to Georgia and was divided into thirteen English colonies.

Three thousand miles of ocean lay between England and her American colonies. Weeks were needed for messages to travel across the Atlantic. The mother country could not possibly make all the laws necessary to carry on the affairs of each little village. The result was that colonial towns and counties elected their own officers and passed laws to manage all small and unimportant matters. This was good practice in the lesson of governing themselves. The people were becoming independent and were learning to decide what laws were right and best for themselves.

Their greatest weakness was that the people of each colony were interested only in their own affairs and knew very little about what was going on in other parts of the country. Very few of the colonial leaders understood how much stronger and better the English colonies would be if they had some way of working together. They thought of themselves as New Yorkers, Pennsylvanians, or Virginians, rather than as Americans.

Benjamin Franklin

One of the wisest of the colonial leaders was Benjamin Franklin, a peaceful citizen of Philadelphia. In 1754, at the beginning of the French and Indian War, he tried to persuade the colonies to unite. A meeting had been called in Albany, New York, for the purpose of making a treaty with the Iroquois Indians. At this meeting Franklin explained a plan by which the different parts of the country could work together. He suggested that each colony elect a few of its best leaders and send them to a congress which should meet once a year. Questions concerning the welfare of the whole country could be talked over and a plan of action decided upon. Unfortunately, most of the colonies saw no need of such a congress, and the king of England did not like the plan because he feared it would give the colonists too

AMERICAN PATRIOTS

much power. Twenty years went by before the colonists were ready to accept Franklin's idea and unite.

Benjamin Franklin has written a very interesting story of his own life. In this book, called his *Autobiography*, he tells of leaving his home in Boston as a poor boy of seventeen, and going to Philadelphia. One Sunday morning, in 1723, he arrived by boat at the foot of Market Street. His clothing was wrinkled and his pockets were stuffed with an extra shirt and a pair of stockings. He had very little money and was hungry; so he bought three large rolls at a baker's shop. Walking up Market Street, he carried one roll under each arm and ate the third one for his breakfast.

Young Franklin was a stranger in a strange city, with nothing to help him but his knowledge of the printing business, his own strong hands, and a determination to work hard and succeed. In a few years he owned and published the *Pennsylvania Gazette*, a weekly newspaper which soon became the best one in the American colonies. In addition to his newspaper, Franklin published an almanac for many years.

In colonial days almanacs took the place of our calendars, but they were bound like magazines. Besides a calendar, the almanac gave a record of tides, the time of the full moon, predictions of the weather, and advice about planting crops. Jokes and short, wise sayings called *proverbs* were scattered through the pages.

Franklin's almanac became very popular. Many children used it for a reader at school and it was translated into other languages. This little book carried his fame into the homes of all the American colonies and even to Europe. People learned to watch for it and to plan their daily lives by it. Franklin pretended that he only printed the almanac, and that a man named Richard Saunders really wrote it. For that reason Franklin called his yearbook *Poor Richard's Almanac*. But before long everyone knew that the funny little articles and wise sayings were really written by the rising young printer of Philadelphia. The people of Franklin's time read his proverbs over and over again until they knew them by heart.

Here are some of these proverbs which we still repeat today:

"A word to the wise is sufficient."

"A bird in the hand is worth two in the bush."

"Never leave that for tomorrow which you can do today."

"Early to bed and early to rise makes a man healthy, wealthy, and wise."

Franklin lived very simply and did many things to improve the city and colony in which he lived. The first paving and street lighting, the first fire and police protection, the first library, a college, and a hospital in Philadelphia were all started through the help of Benjamin Franklin. Franklin also invented the first good oil lamp, and made a stove to be used instead of an open fireplace. He discovered that lightning is electricity in the sky, and he made the first lightning rod.

In France and England, as well as in America, Franklin became well known and greatly admired. When the colonists of Pennsylvania needed a man of ability and good judgment to manage their business affairs in England, Benjamin Franklin was asked to go. Thus it happened that this wise leader was far away during some of the most important years of colonial history.

Duty of American Colonies Toward England

The end of the French and Indian War in 1763 brought great rejoicing. For nine years, colonial soldiers had fought side by side with the trained troops from England. The American colonies were proud of the mother country and glad that they could help in winning this great new tract of land for England. Hardly anyone even thought of an independent nation in the New World. Yet in twelve years the American colonists were once more at war, and this time they were fighting against the English soldiers instead of with them.

The trouble which led to the Revolutionary War was caused chiefly by King George III and the men whom he chose to take charge of American affairs. Many of the people of England did not approve of the war, and sided openly with the colonists. William Pitt, the great English statesman, was a friend of America and did all that he could to get the English Government to treat her colonies fairly.

From the time of the first settlement at Jamestown, the English kings and the American settlers had never agreed about the rights and duties of colonies. The colonists thought that they should be allowed to trade and do business with anyone for their own profit just like the people in England. The kings had always said, "It is the duty of every colony to help the mother country. What is the use of owning colonies if they do not bring a rich trade to England?"

Trade laws, called *Navigation Acts*, were made in England to force the American colonists to trade only with the mother country. One law said that all goods taken to or from the colonies must be carried in English or colonial ships. Another gave a list of colonial products such as sugar, cotton, and tobacco which must be sold only in England. Many of the useful things which the colonists needed were made in England. In order to compel them to buy these things from English merchants, a law forbade the colonists to make and sell them in America.

In spite of the grumbling about these laws, the colonists had no thought of rebelling openly against the English Government. But the Navigation Acts were often disobeyed. Ships from the French and Spanish West Indies continued to carry sugar, molasses, rice, and ginger to American merchants, and to take back goods which had been made in New England. There were not enough English officers to guard the coast, and these things could easily be smuggled into and out of the colonies.

In spite of the unpopular laws, the mother country and her colonies were still on friendly terms. Prosperous colonial families wanted to buy many things which were made in England, and a good trade went on steadily between England and America.

The Quarrel Begins

At the close of the French and Indian War, England needed a great deal of money. King George III and his officers decided that the war had given the colonies much valuable new land and that therefore these colonies ought to help pay the British debts of the war. The colonies insisted that they had raised and supported more than their share of the troops. In order to collect the money, the English Government tried to compel the colonists to obey the Navigation Acts. Ships were sent to guard the coast, and English officers were told to arrest and fine any colonist found with smuggled goods. This was not an easy order to carry out. Smuggling became more dangerous, but on many a dark night, boats landed at some lonely part of the coast, and forbidden goods were safely hidden away before daylight.

In order to help the officers, the English Government decided to allow the use of Writs of Assistance. These were papers from the court, giving permission to enter and search a man's house. If a colonist was suspected of storing smuggled goods, an officer secured a Writ of Assistance and searched the suspected man's house from attic to cellar. The people became very angry when they were compelled to stand by and see their property overhauled by the king's officers.

The New England colonies carried on most of the American manufacture and trade, and they suffered most from the Navigation Acts and the Writs of Assistance. The busy port of Boston became the very center of the growing quarrel with England.

Another plan which the king carried out was to keep an army of British soldiers in the colonies. He said that these troops were sent to protect the colonists from attacks by Indians, and from their French and Spanish neighbors. But the colonists did not want the troops. They had always taken care of themselves, and they feared that the real reason for an army in America was to compel them to obey the trade laws.

Matters became much worse when a law called the *Stamp Act* was passed in 1765. The purpose of this law was to tax the colonists for money to pay for the army. The king and his officers could not have chosen a surer way of making open trouble with the colonists. The Stamp Act declared that every business paper must bear a government stamp in order to be recognized in court as a true and legal paper. This meant that no colonist could buy or sell property, lease his farm or store, make a will, or be married without buying the English stamps. Even newspapers and almanacs must be printed on stamped paper. This law affected all the colonies equally, and the entire country was angry at this tax.

These American citizens knew that taxes were necessary and right. No government could be carried on without money to pay its expenses. Each year their own assemblies voted taxes to keep up roads and schools, to pay the officers and soldiers who protected their homes, and to provide for all the other needs of their colonies. But the members of these assemblies were elected by the people. In the different colonies quarrels often arose between the assemblies and the royal governors sent from England. But the people's assemblies had always succeeded in keeping the privilege of deciding on the kind and amount of taxes to be collected from the people.

England soon found that she had undertaken a hard task when she attempted to collect taxes from the colonists by the sale of stamps. Meetings were held in all parts of the country and angry speeches were made, urging the people to refuse to buy the stamps.

The Orator of the Revolution

News of the Stamp Act caused great excitement in the people's assembly of Virginia. A new member was attending the assembly for the first time. He was Patrick Henry, a young Virginia lawyer who was said to be a powerful speaker. For some time he listened in silence while the members of the assembly spoke on the subject of the Stamp Act. But Patrick Henry was not at all satisfied with the words which he heard. Some of the members were wealthy planters who sold their cotton and tobacco in England. Trouble with the mother country would interfere with their business, and they hoped that this dispute might be settled peacefully. One of these men advised writing a friendly letter to England telling how much the colonists objected to the Stamp Act.

During this man's speech Patrick Henry tore a blank page from a law book and hurriedly wrote a statement of the rights which he believed all colonists should have. At the first chance he arose and began to speak. The others watched the new member with curiosity, but soon his fiery words compelled their entire attention, and many found themselves agreeing with his arguments. He read the resolutions which he had written, and urged the assembly to have them printed in the papers as a public statement of the beliefs of the colony of Virginia.

A lively debate followed, and Patrick Henry made a second great speech. His words became so bold that some of the king's friends shouted, "Treason! treason!" But Henry calmly finished his talk even though he knew that he could be imprisoned and even put to death if treason could be proved against him. At the end of his speech the assembly was in an uproar, but when the votes were counted, the resolutions were found to have passed. The cause of liberty had found a leader in Virginia. For many years, Patrick Henry continued to stir the country with his burning words. Now we call him the "Orator of the Revolution."

The Colonists Resist the Stamp Act

In time of trouble it was natural for the colonies to turn to each other for help. The leaders of Massachusetts suggested that a congress be held, so that all the colonies could unite in sending a petition to the English king to ask his help in repealing the Stamp Act. This meeting was held in New York in 1765 and was called the Stamp Act Congress.

In the meantime, Samuel Adams, one of the leaders of Massachusetts, wrote resolutions like those of Patrick Henry, which were adopted by the Massachusetts Assembly. He also wrote friendly letters to many of the prominent men of England. In one of these he suggested that the Americans might refuse to buy goods from English merchants until the Stamp Act was repealed. This idea was quickly taken up by the colonists. It was printed in newspapers and written in letters until it spread from one end of the country to the other. Everywhere people pledged themselves to buy nothing from England while the Stamp Act was in force.

The first of November came, the day on which stamps must begin to be used. Every effort of the colonists to have the law repealed had failed. Stamps were sent to America, and officers were appointed to sell them. Business immediately came to a standstill, for no one would buy the stamps. The young men in many of the colonies formed clubs and called themselves the Sons of Liberty. In North Carolina seven hundred Sons of Liberty surrounded the governor's house and would not leave until the stamp officer resigned. In other towns the stamps were stolen and burned, and in many places the English officers were threatened until they gave up their positions.

Benjamin Franklin, who was still in England, did all that he could to help the colonists. He called on many of the leaders of Parliament and urged them to work for the repeal of the Stamp Act.

Even these efforts met with no success until the English merchants discovered that their trade was falling off. When they saw that the colonists were really keeping their pledge not to buy goods from England, these merchants insisted that Parliament take some action to improve matters. The king then sent for Benjamin Franklin and asked him many questions about conditions in America. Franklin told him that the colonists would never

AMERICAN PATRIOTS

consent to buy the stamps, and after much arguing and debate, the hated law finally was repealed.

The colonists were very happy. They felt that this action showed that their king and the mother country wished to treat them fairly after all. They celebrated their joy by ringing bells, feasting, and drinking the health of the king. In Virginia and New York, statues of the king were thrown down and many of the Sons of Liberty clubs disbanded.

Growing Trouble in the Colonies

In the general rejoicing very few people paid any attention to a statement which Parliament made when the Stamp Act was repealed. The statement said that England had the right to make laws for "the colonies and people of America, subjects of the crown of Great Britain, in all cases whatsoever." Thoughtful leaders realized that those last words meant that the king still claimed the right to tax the colonists. The whole country soon realized that this was true. During the next year, 1767, a tax was placed on all glass, paper, paints, and tea which were shipped to America. Parliament said that all Navigation Acts must be obeyed, and the officers were told to use the Writs of Assistance.

Once more the colonies were aroused, and Samuel Adams spent hours at his desk writing letters to prominent men in England. He told them that the people in America believed that "taxation without representation is tyranny." This meant that the

222 ENGLAND AND HER COLONIES

English Parliament had no right to tax the colonies, because there was not a single member who had been elected in America and sent to the English Parliament to represent the colonists. Some people felt that this difficulty could easily be remedied, but Adams explained that London was too far away to think of sending such representatives. This was quite true. In 1767, the telephone, the telegraph, and the radio were unknown. Messages traveled so slowly that an American member of Parliament could not know how the people for whom he was acting would want him to vote.

The colonists had many friends in England. William Pitt led the group in Parliament that sided with the Americans. They argued fearlessly against the taxes. But the king and his officers continued to have their own way. When Samuel Adams found that there was no hope of help in England, he wrote a letter and sent it to the peoples' assembly in every colony. This became known as the "Circular Letter." It angered the king because Adams suggested that all the colonies stand by each other and form a plan for opposing these unjust laws.

The English officers in America found the new taxes very hard to collect, and more soldiers were sent to help them. Two regiments arrived in Boston, and the sight of these Redcoats on the streets made the citizens more angry. There was constant trouble between the colonists and the soldiers. During one of their quarrels, five Americans were killed and several wounded. The Americans called this event the Boston Massacre, and when the news of it spread throughout the colonies, people became much alarmed.

On the same day an important thing happened in England. The king had been surprised to find that it cost the mother country far more to collect her

The sight of the Redcoats in Boston made the citizens angry

taxes in America than she was getting back. Something must be done. At last all the taxes were withdrawn except the one on tea. These rebellious people, they thought, must be made to understand that England had the right to tax her colonies. Therefore, this one tax was kept. At the same time the price of tea was made so low that it cost less in America than in England.

King George III and his friends expected to trick the colonists into paying a tax, but they had no idea how strong the feeling in America had become. Samuel Adams formed a Committee of Correspondence in Massachusetts, and similar committees were started in other towns and colonies. Letters telling what was happening in different parts of the country passed back and forth, and everywhere people pledged themselves not to use any tea.

In the meantime shiploads of tea were on their way to America. What was to be done with it? In South Carolina, the tea was landed but no one would buy any; so it was stored in damp cellars and much of it spoiled. In Philadelphia and New York the ships were not allowed to land, and they sailed back to England taking the tea with them.

The greatest excitement was in Boston. Three English ships loaded with tea lay in the harbor waiting for permission either to unload their cargoes or to take it back to England. A meeting of the citizens was called on December 16, 1773, and Samuel Adams took charge of the meeting. All the stores were closed and people crowded into the famous Old South Church. Here they voted that the tea should not be landed and sent a message to the royal governor, asking for the proper papers so that the captain could sail back to England. The governor refused. Most of the day was spent in efforts to send the ships peacefully away.

AMERICAN PATRIOTS

At last, soon after darkness had fallen on that short winter day, Samuel Adams arose and said, "This meeting can do nothing more to save the country." As these words were spoken, a war whoop was heard outside and a band of men dressed as Mohawk Indians rushed by. They hurried to the ships, opened every chest of tea on board, and emptied it into Boston Harbor.

This Boston Tea Party was a lawless act, and brought much trouble to the city. In England many of the friends of America turned against them and Boston was in disgrace. The king and his friends were determined to punish the rebellious city. Laws were passed saying that Boston must pay for the tea, and that until this was done and they promised to obey the laws, no ship could enter or leave their port. Town meetings could not be held except with the consent of the king's governor, and everyone arrested for a crime must be sent to England or to another colony for trial.

Drifting Toward War

The colonists were alarmed by these laws. They felt that now they must unite in an effort to have their rights respected. In September, 1774, leaders from all the colonies met at Philadelphia. There they formed the First Continental Congress, and definitely planned to work together. Many were not in favor of war, yet there seemed no chance for a peaceful settlement of their troubles. In every colony there were also many citizens, called *Tories*, who sided with the king and felt that England had a right to make any laws that she wished for her colonies. But the greater number were determined to resist the unjust taxes, and a few began to hope for an independent country, altogether free from England.

After the First Continental Congress, citizens in every colony began to collect guns and ammunition, and men began to drill and prepare themselves for war. Companies of soldiers called *minutemen* were formed. The name meant that these men had pledged themselves to drop their work and go to the defense of the country at any minute. The Sons of Liberty were very active. They watched the king's governors, the tax officers, and the British soldiers, and reported all that they heard to the Committees of Correspondence. Many letters traveled back and forth. In Virginia, Patrick Henry delivered his greatest speech, ending with the famous words, "I know not what course others may take; but as for me, give me liberty or give me death."

Samuel Adams and another patriot named John Hancock knew that they were in danger of being arrested and sent to England for trial on a charge of treason. Therefore they left Boston and carried on their work at the small town of Lexington. The colonists were collecting stores of guns and ammunition at the neighboring town of Concord. Then a

AMERICAN PATRIOTS

Paul Revere raced through the night on his famous ride

day came when one of the Sons of Liberty learned that the British were about to arrest the two leaders and capture the stores at Concord.

The king's troops were secretly watched. Near midnight on April 18, 1775, they began quiet preparations for the march to Lexington and Concord. One of the Sons of Liberty who was on guard waited until he was sure that the British would march by land. Then he hurried to the Old North Church and hung a lantern in the tower. Across the Charles River waited the messenger, Paul Revere. This lantern was his signal. The moment it appeared, Paul Revere leaped to his saddle and raced through the night on his famous ride. Every citizen along the way was warned that the British were coming.

At dawn, the British reached Lexington. Samuel Adams and John Hancock had fled, but there on the village common was drawn up a brave little band of sixty minutemen. Here the first gun of the Revolutionary War was fired, on April 19, 1775.

The colonists were scattered, and the British went on to capture the supplies at Concord. There they found that most of the guns and ammunition had been taken away by the colonists, and they turned back to Boston. Minutemen hidden behind trees and fences fired at the Redcoats as they passed. Many were killed and the rest were glad to reach

Minutemen fired at the Redcoats as they passed

the shelter of Boston. At last the long quarrel between England and her colonies had ended in war.

News of the fighting at Lexington and Concord spread quickly from town to town. Messengers on swift horses were sent to the neighboring colonies. At each inn where the horsemen stopped, the story of the battle caused great excitement. At last the news reached the cities of New York, Pennsylvania,

AMERICAN PATRIOTS

and Virginia, and even the small settlements of the West and South. Everywhere, patriotic colonists began to collect arms and to drill small forces of volunteer soldiers. Colonial soldiers, hastily gathering from all parts of New England, guarded the city of Boston, where the British soldiers were staying.

On May 10, 1775, about three weeks after the battle of Lexington, leaders from all the colonies met at Philadelphia in the Second Continental Congress. Many serious problems faced the members of this Congress. The colonies were already at war with England, but they had no united government to guide them. They could not hope to protect themselves against a powerful enemy like England unless they worked together. The Second Continental Congress, therefore, formed itself into a government to rule the United Colonies of America.

Congress had also to raise an army, for fighting had already begun. The soldiers who were gathering around Boston were taken as the beginning of an American army, and Congress asked every colony to raise troops and furnish supplies to help defend the country.

Who should be commander in chief of the new army? Where could a leader be found, wise and strong enough to form the rough colonial soldiers into a successful army? Many of the members of Congress thought of the brave Virginia soldier who had proved his ability in the French and Indian

230 ENGLAND AND HER COLONIES

War. They decided to ask George Washington to be commander in chief.

REPORTING ON A TOPIC

This chapter is very interesting. You have heard and read about many of its topics before.

See how well you can do in a talk to your group on some of these topics. Choose at least three, and be prepared to talk about each for at least one minute without having anyone ask questions.

Such a report is a summary, but to it you should add anything that will make your talk interesting.

On the map in your geography, find the seacoast from Maine to Georgia where the thirteen colonies were located.

Name one of the colonies where the land was best suited for farming. What were the most important products?

What colonies became noted for their trade and shipbuilding?

THE REVOLUTIONARY WAR
GEORGE WASHINGTON
Early Training of George Washington

In front of the inn in the little Virginia village of Fredericksburg were several visitors talking to the innkeeper. As they stood there, a tall, fair-haired boy came out of the near-by general store, mounted a waiting horse, and galloped away down the street.

"How that boy rides!" said one of the strangers. "Who is he?"

"Oh, he's one of the Washington boys from across the river," the innkeeper replied. "George, they call him. All the Washingtons are good riders, and George comes up to the family mark."

While the innkeeper told his guests about the Washingtons, George was riding homeward. He always enjoyed the trip to Fredericksburg and wished that the road were longer. All too soon he reached his home. He had much to do, for although he was only thirteen, he was the oldest boy at home, and he helped to manage the work of the plantation. His father had died when George was eleven, and his two older brothers, Lawrence and Augustine, had farms of their own.

George spent much of his time with his older brothers. There was no good school in Fredericksburg;

so he lived with one of them in order to keep on with his studies. One of his teachers was a skilful woodsman, and from him the young student probably learned to measure and survey land. He loved this kind of work and did it well. By the time he was sixteen, he could survey land as well as his teacher.

Near Lawrence Washington's plantation lived a rich English nobleman, Lord Fairfax. He and young George Washington became very good friends. Lord Fairfax owned a great tract of wild land farther to the west, whose boundaries had never been marked. He felt that his young sixteen-year-old friend could be trusted to measure his land correctly. So he hired George Washington and two other men to make the survey.

For a month the little party lived in the woods far from all colonial settlements. Sometimes the men were fortunate enough to find the cabin of a friendly settler where they could spend the night. The settler's cabins were few, and usually the surveyors built a camp fire, rolled up in their blankets near the fire, and slept on the damp ground. It was spring, and rains and melting snow turned the rivers into raging torrents. When the men reached a stream which must be crossed, they sometimes had to force the frightened horses to swim to the other shore. Often their clothing was wet and cold for days at a time.

George Washington stood the hardships well. In a month the survey was completed, and the men

GEORGE WASHINGTON

returned and made their report to Lord Fairfax. The English nobleman was much pleased, and he praised the young surveyor so much that others began to hear about him.

The next year George Washington was appointed county surveyor for a large tract of wild land in Virginia. With this important work to do for the colony, he was often in the woods for weeks at a time. He became acquainted with Indians and learned how to deal with them wisely. The rough life taught him to endure hardships and dangers. It prepared him for a time of which he did not dream — when he would lead an army on long hard marches.

Soon he was having other training for a soldier's life. His brother Lawrence had been a soldier in the English army, and George had often longed to become a soldier too. Lawrence was now very ill, but before he died, he did what he could for his younger brother. Partly through Lawrence's efforts, George was appointed a major in the Virginia colonial troops called the *militia*. Two army friends of Lawrence's taught George Washington how to drill his soldiers.

Early Services for His Country

Meanwhile, the quarrel between France and England over their American lands was rapidly moving toward war. Word reached Governor Dinwiddie of Virginia that the French were building forts along the Ohio River on land which England claimed as part of her colony of Virginia. A message must be sent to these French soldiers warning them to leave the country.

The messenger chosen for this errand would have to travel through the unbroken wilderness across the Appalachian Mountains. The journey would require a strong, fearless woodsman who would use good judgment in delivering his message and would learn everything possible about the plans of the French.

George Washington was at this time only twenty-one years old, but he was already known as a trained woodsman and one of the most dependable young soldiers of Virginia. Governor Dinwiddie chose him to make this important journey into the Ohio country.

The same day that the message was given to him, George Washington, with a few companions, set out for the French forts. It was late in the autumn of 1753, and a hard winter journey lay before the messengers. There were no roads. The men had to find their way through the wilderness as best they could. Great snowstorms made travel difficult, and enemy Indians added to the dangers.

Washington was used to hardships like these and successfully made the journey. He delivered his letter to the French commander and brought back a reply. The reply told Governor Dinwiddie very little, but Washington had seen and heard enough

GEORGE WASHINGTON

to know that the French did not mean to give up the land. He saw that England must defend her claims if she wanted to hold the Ohio River valley, and that war with the French was very near.

Soon the fighting began between the French and the English. Washington helped to defend the frontier during most of the French and Indian War. He became an experienced soldier and commander, well-known in other colonies besides Virginia.

In 1759, Washington left the army and went home to the farm he had inherited from his brother Lawrence, Mount Vernon on the Potomac River. He was glad to settle down to the peaceful life of a plantation owner. The work of the plantation prospered. At the docks of England and the West Indies, many a barrel of flour and tobacco was unloaded, bearing the mark "George Washington, Mount Vernon, Virginia."

Soon Washington was elected a member of the Virginia assembly, or House of Burgesses. He was present during the excitement caused by news of the Stamp Act. He heard the great speeches of Patrick Henry and helped to pass the resolutions which declared that England had no right to tax her colonies. He listened thoughtfully to the news of all the alarming events which were occurring in Boston.

When the First Continental Congress met in 1774, at Philadelphia, Washington was there as one of the representatives from Virginia. He met many of the leaders of the other colonies and learned how strong was the feeling against the British taxes. When he went home, he began drilling his colonial soldiers, for he felt that soon they might be needed.

The fighting at Lexington and Concord brought the colonies closer together than they had ever been before. When the Second Continental Congress met in Philadelphia, on May 10, 1775, the foremost leaders of the colonies were there. Benjamin Franklin, just home from England, attended the meetings, and Samuel Adams, John Hancock, Patrick Henry, and George Washington were among the delegates.

Washington Becomes Commander in Chief

The men of the Congress agreed that George Washington was the wisest and most experienced military leader in the colonies. However, when they asked him to become the commander in chief of the new Continental army, he did not accept at once. He doubted his own ability to lead the army successfully. Finally, after he had decided that his duty was to serve the colonies as their commander in chief, he arose and said, "I beg it may be remembered by every gentleman in this room, that I this day declare, with the utmost sincerity, I do not think myself equal to the command I am honored with."

Since the army was near Boston, General Washington rode to that city to take command of the troops. Before he arrived, news reached him that a battle had been fought at Bunker Hill, just outside Boston. Twice the British soldiers had tried to take the hill, and twice the brave patriots turned them back. At the third attack the colonial troops gave way because they had no more ammunition.

Although the British won, the battle showed that untrained colonial soldiers could stand against the British regular army. The people were greatly encouraged, and Washington exclaimed, "The liberties of the country are safe!"

When Washington took command of the army, many of the men were still wearing their homespun suits and carrying the rifles which had hung on their kitchen walls at home. They were men rough in appearance and untrained in war, but they were brave and determined. Moreover, they were more skilful with the rifle than any other troops in the world. All during the summer of 1775 and the following winter, Washington drilled them and trained them. By the spring of 1776, Washington felt that he had a Continental army, ready to carry on the war.

In March, 1776, Washington made his first move by taking possession of Dorchester Heights, just south of Boston. The guns of the Continental army could now be fired on the British army in Boston. General Howe, the English commander, found that he must either fight or retreat. He could not risk a battle, so he put his troops on board English ships and sailed away to Canada.

The Declaration of Independence

By this time, the idea of complete separation and independence from England had grown strong in the minds of many Colonials. King George III had refused to listen to their petitions. He had called them rebels, sent his soldiers to punish them, and was even hiring Hessian troops from Germany to fight against them. More and more, the colonists were thinking of independence.

At last Richard Henry Lee of Virginia arose in Congress and made the motion, "That these United Colonies are, and of right ought to be, free and independent States." Congress was not ready to vote on so important a matter at once. It appointed Thomas Jefferson from Virginia, Benjamin Franklin, Philip Livingston, John Adams, and Roger Sherman to write a Declaration of Independence. When the Declaration was ready, it was presented to Congress for adoption.

Every member of the Continental Congress felt that an important decision must now be made. If the vote was cast for independence, the colonies must face a war with England. Defeat in the war would bring ruin to the country and to the defeated colonists. After a long debate, the Declaration of Independence was adopted on July 4, 1776.

News of the Declaration of Independence was received with rejoicing. In every village bells rang, cannons boomed, and people crowded together to hear the Declaration read.

GEORGE WASHINGTON

But not all the colonists approved of what had been done. Some believed that King George had a perfect right to make whatever laws he wished for his colonies. Many disliked the unjust trade laws and taxes and were willing to fight for their rights, but they wanted to remain Englishmen. They did not want to separate from England. When the Declaration of Independence was signed by representatives from all the colonies, every citizen had to choose on which side he would stand. Those who remained loyal to England — and they were many — were called *Tories*. As the war went on, they did much to help the English army and to hinder the cause of independence in America.

Hard Times for the Colonies

During the excitement over the Declaration of Independence, General Washington went quietly on with his preparations for war. He knew that the natural water route from Canada along Lake Champlain and the Hudson River, with New York as the gateway, would play an important part in the war for the independence of the colonies. If the English could form a line of strong forts along this route, the rebellious colonies of New England would be cut off from the rest of the country. The English could then conquer each part separately. In order to prevent them from carrying out this plan, Washington moved his army to Long Island. He fortified the western end of the island and built a fort on each side of the Hudson River above the city of New York.

The Continental army was not strong enough to hold New York. General Howe collected more troops and supplies in Canada and hurried to Long Island with a strong British force. Washington's brave little army was defeated in battle at the western end of Long Island, opposite the city of New York.

But the Colonials had a leader who knew how to face defeat. As darkness came after the battle was over, General Howe thought that he had the "ragged rebels" neatly trapped on Long Island. A strong northeast wind was blowing, so he delayed sailing up the East River. He could easily capture the rebels in the morning he thought. During the night the wind went down and a heavy fog hid the Colonials as they slipped quietly away in small boats and landed on Manhattan Island above New York. The "ragged rebels" had excaped from the trap. General Washington had to leave the important city of New York to the British. But the Colonials stood guard above the city to try to prevent the English from going up the Hudson River.

Meanwhile, more troops, well-trained and well-equipped, were arriving from England. Hessian soldiers hired from Germany also came to fight in the British army. In the fall of 1776, British forces were sent to capture Philadelphia, the capital of the

GEORGE WASHINGTON

colonies. Washington had to divide his army. Leaving part of his troops to watch the Hudson River, he hurried into New Jersey with the rest. There he succeeded in getting between Philadelphia and the British forces. But his little army could not hope to win against the strong, well-trained troops of England. Slowly he retreated, delaying the enemy as much as possible.

Each day the country expected news of a battle. At last the British troops were only thirty miles from Philadelphia, and still the retreat continued. The colonial army reached the Delaware River with the British close behind them. Washington ordered every boat for miles up and down the river to be collected. Then the Colonials crossed the river, taking the boats with them. When the British arrived on the eastern shore, they were stopped for lack of boats. Winter was beginning, and ice would soon form in the river. Then, thought the British commander, the crossing would be easy. So the British went into camp in several New Jersey towns and waited for freezing weather.

Washington's army was safe for a time, but things looked very dark for the cause of the colonies. The soldiers were discouraged because they saw no prospect of a victory. Their clothing was thin and ragged. Their food was scarce and poor. They had not been paid even the small wages which colonial soldiers usually received. Many of the men had enlisted for only a year, and as soon as their time was up, they insisted upon going home. In spite of all that Washington could do, his army was steadily growing smaller. Even the people at home complained and criticized. "Why," they asked, "does Washington never fight? Does he think he can win the war by running away?"

Washington himself was doing much to help the cause for which he was working. When the Continental Congress made him the commander in chief, he had refused all pay except for his most necessary expenses. Now, when his men were suffering, Washington did all that he could to provide for them. His own needs came last. Many times he wrote letters to Congress, begging them to send supplies more promptly. He secured some help for his army from wealthy men of the country. He himself was a wealthy man, and he used much of his own money to provide clothing and food for the men, and to pay them in order that their families at home might be cared for.

Fighting for Freedom

In the midst of the gloom and discouragement, one of the chances came for which Washington was constantly watching. It was Christmas night, in 1776. Hessian soldiers in Trenton, New Jersey, were celebrating the day with feasting. They felt perfectly safe, for the Delaware River was full of dangerous floating ice and Washington was on the other side. Snow was falling in a blinding storm.

GEORGE WASHINGTON 243

Washington's surprise attack on Trenton resulted in the capture of the enemy's men and supplies

Suddenly shouting was heard outside and messengers broke up the gay parties with cries of "The rebels are coming, the rebels are coming."

The Hessians rushed out to find their only way of escape held by the Colonials. Washington had collected rowboats and with a small force had crossed the dangerous river to surprise the enemy at Trenton. The attack was successful, and prisoners and supplies were captured. A few days later Lord Cornwallis, leader of the British army in New Jersey, was surprised and defeated at Princeton. The British army marched back to New York to spend the rest of the winter.

These two successes encouraged the whole country. In England, the king and his friends began to see that this war against the colonies would not be so short and easy as they had expected. The king's secretary for colonial affairs said afterward, "All our hopes were blasted by that unhappy affair at Trenton." But the king was determined to conquer the rebellious colonies. Plans were made for a strong campaign in America, and more troops and supplies were sent.

General Washington continued to use his small army so skilfully that he escaped capture and yet hindered and annoyed the British at every turn. In spite of all that he could do, however, General Howe captured Philadelphia in September, 1777. The loss of Philadelphia was a heavy blow to the colonists, but soon good news of a victory in the north encouraged them.

A British army under General Burgoyne was invading the country from Canada, using the well-known route along Lake Champlain and the Hudson River. General Howe had been expected to move up the Hudson River from New York to meet Burgoyne. If they could cut off the New England colonies, they would win the war. But through some mistake, Howe was already fighting his way into Philadelphia at the time when he should have been starting north.

At first Burgoyne was successful. He led a large army of well-trained British soldiers, and many Indians from Canada came with him. They captured American forts along the way, and pushed on to the Hudson River.

In the meantime the militia of New York and the New England colonies were hastily gathering at Albany, and many new volunteers were joining them. They were all brave men who were determined to protect their homes from this invading army. Washington sent General Gates with a small troop to take charge of these combined forces. They marched north and met Burgoyne at Saratoga, where two successful battles were fought.

The British general would have been glad to retreat to Canada, but his way was now blocked by strong forces of militia from Vermont and New Hampshire. These bold backwoodsmen had hurried into New York at the rear of Burgoyne's army. He was hemmed in on all sides, and his food was giving out. On October 17, 1777, he surrendered his entire army.

The colonists were overjoyed. The British defeat at Saratoga meant that England's plan of dividing the colonies had failed. Even more important was another result of the battle, a result which took place in France.

Franklin Seeks Help from France

Soon after the Declaration of Independence was signed, the Continental Congress had sent Benjamin Franklin to France. Congress hoped that he could persuade the French Government to help the colonies in their war against England.

Franklin was the right man for the task. His almanac and his experiments with electricity had made him better known in Europe than any other American. In Paris Franklin quickly won the friendship of the French people. They liked his quick wit and his simple, friendly manner. Before long they were heartily in sympathy with the cause of the colonies. Many of the young nobles of France offered to leave their homes and fight side by side with the Continentals to help them win their independence. One of these whose name will always be remembered was the Marquis de Lafayette. He became an officer in the Continental army and did much to help the colonies in their struggle.

Franklin also won the friendship of the government of France. But the king hesitated to recognize the colonies as a new nation. If they were defeated in their war for independence, he feared that France might find herself in trouble with England.

GEORGE WASHINGTON

At last came the news that General Burgoyne had surrendered to the Continental army. The people in Paris celebrated the event as though it had been a great French victory, and the French Government was ready to help the colonies openly. A few weeks after the news arrived, Franklin succeeded in making a treaty of friendship between France and the United Colonies of America. The French Government agreed to lend money to the Continental Congress, and to send armies and warships to help the struggling colonial army.

This joyful news reached Washington near the end of the hardest winter which his army had spent. They were encamped at Valley Forge in Pennsylvania. Not far away, General Howe's army was enjoying the comfort of Philadelphia. At Valley Forge, however, the Continental troops were suffering from cold and hunger. Congress had no money for supplies, and Washington, in spite of all his efforts, could not provide the food, clothing, and blankets which were needed. On the coldest nights the men did not try to sleep, but sat around their camp fires to keep warm. Many became sick and died. All proved themselves real heroes by patiently enduring the hardships of that dreadful winter.

When England heard of the treaty with France, she offered to make peace with the colonies and to grant them everything which they asked except independence. The colonies would not consider the offer. With the help of France, they now felt sure of success and were determined to continue their struggle for independence.

France kept her promises of help, but in spite of her aid, the war dragged on for three more years. General Howe left Philadelphia and returned to New York. Washington followed him and remained near the city to protect the Hudson River district and the surrounding towns.

Fighting in the South

Much of the fighting now went on in the South, for the British were trying a new plan. They intended to start in Georgia and move north, conquering one colony after another. They hoped at least to save for England the rich tobacco, rice, and cotton colonies of the South.

The plan was successful for a time. Georgia and most of South Carolina were conquered by the British. At one time the Continental army in South Carolina seemed entirely destroyed. But volunteer leaders gathered small bands of devoted followers, who hid in the forests and swamps. The most noted of these leaders was Francis Marion. His men were bold and skilful horsemen who could use their rifles well. They followed the British troops, hiding and watching until a small group of the enemy were sent to gather food supplies. This gave them an opportunity which was never wasted. Riding like the wind, they surprised the British, killed or scattered the soldiers, and captured their supplies. When things looked darkest for the colonists in the South, these lawless fighters kept the cause of independence alive until good generals with new troops arrived from the North.

The Surrender at Yorktown

All during the Revolutionary War, the British in America had to face two great difficulties. First, they could not conquer a district and leave it to remain conquered. As soon as the British army marched away, the people became once more the independent citizens that life in America had taught them to be. The second difficulty was that British troops were fighting far from home. All their supplies, especially ammunition, had to be brought by ships from England. For this reason, British generals had to return often to the coast and keep in close touch with their ships.

Washington had long been patiently waiting for a chance to trap the British and cut them off from their supplies. At last the opportunity came.

In the South, General Greene's small force of Continentals were in retreat. Lord Cornwallis and his army had been following them northward. The two armies had marched entirely across the western part of North Carolina. At length Cornwallis turned toward the sea. In Virginia, Lafayette was at the head of a small Continental force. He skilfully kept near Cornwallis but avoided the necessity of fighting. The two armies marched back and forth like men in a great game of chess, each trying to corner the other. At last Cornwallis again turned toward the coast and went into camp at Yorktown. This town was on a narrow strip of land at the mouth of the James River. Many years before, Captain John Smith and the first English colonists had settled near this very place.

Cornwallis felt safe. Back of him was Chesapeake Bay. British ships could keep his army well supplied, and he could sail away if he must. From the higher ground near by, Lafayette watched the British army and sent word to Washington, describing the position of both forces.

When the news came, Washington was still on the Hudson River, standing guard over the British army in New York. He knew that his great chance had come and he acted quickly. He had just received an offer from the French to make use of their fleet near the West Indies. He now sent a message asking the French admiral to go with all speed to Yorktown, drive away the British ships, and guard the coast where Cornwallis was in camp.

Part of his army Washington ordered to make a great show of attacking New York in order to keep General Clinton from sending help to Cornwallis.

Events in the Revolutionary War

Then with as many Colonial and French troops as possible, he hurried to Yorktown. Before Cornwallis knew what was happening, he was surrounded. Yorktown, which had seemed a safe camp, had become a trap. Before him stood a strong enemy. Behind him Chesapeake Bay was held by French warships instead of by his own friendly English vessels. Two attacks, one by the French under Lafayette, and the other by the Continental army, showed Cornwallis that he could not fight his way through. At last, on October 19, 1781, he surrendered his entire army.

This was the last important fighting of the war. Both sides realized that General Washington had brought victory to the American cause by his success at Yorktown. British troops were removed from the southern cities. But General Clinton's army remained in New York; so Washington returned to his old position on the Hudson River and to his old duty of watching the British troops. Then followed a long wait while the treaty of peace between England and her victorious colonies was being made at Paris.

Peace

Congress sent Benjamin Franklin, John Adams, and John Jay to represent the United Colonies in Paris and to gain the best terms possible for them. The treaty of peace was finally signed in 1783 and was called the Peace of Paris. England agreed to the independence of the thirteen American colonies, and gave up her claims to all the land east of the Mississippi River, from Canada on the north to Florida on the south.

The twenty-fifth of November, 1783, was a day of rejoicing in New York City. The British army was leaving America, and Washington and his

Washington and his troops entered New York with flags flying and bands playing

troops were to march in and take possession of the town. Early in the morning the streets were filled with excited crowds, eager to see all that was going on. The Redcoats marched to the docks at the lower end of the city, where boats were ready to take them to the waiting ships. Then General Washington and the governor of New York, leading a procession of Colonial troops, entered the city with flags flying and bands playing. The day was given up to feasting and celebration.

A few days later, General Washington said good-by to the last of his soldiers and sent them to their homes. He himself had one more duty which must be performed. He went to Congress, made a careful report of the work which he had done, and resigned his commission as commander in chief of the army. Then with a grateful heart he set out for his peaceful home at Mount Vernon.

From United Colonies to United States

But Washington saw that the dangers to the United Colonies were not all over when the war was won. There was really no United States. There were thirteen separate colonies. As long as they were fighting a common enemy, they tried to work together. Now that the war was won, each colony thought mainly of its own interest.

The same year that Cornwallis surrendered at Yorktown, the Articles of Confederation went into effect. These articles were supposed to provide a way for the colonies to work together as a nation. In fact they made a government which was so weak that the wise leaders of the country saw that the Articles of Confederation were of little use.

Under these articles, Congress could ask the states for money. But it had no power to make them furnish it. Congress could not pay the soldiers who had won the war. Neither could it do the many other things that must be done by all the states together rather than by separate states.

To make matters worse, some of the states began to charge a tax or duty on anything brought in from other states. For example, New York taxed a man who brought firewood from Connecticut or one who brought food from New Jersey. Such taxes were the cause of many disputes. The colonies began to be jealous and angry at one another. This of course made it still harder for them to work together.

The wisest leaders like Washington and Franklin soon began to try to form a stronger central government. But it was not until 1787, about six years after the surrender of Cornwallis, that the real work of forming the present United States Government was begun.

The men who built this government met in Independence Hall in Philadelphia. Washington was president of the convention. After a long, hard struggle, the Constitution of the United States was written.

It then had to be accepted, or adopted by the states. This meant that there were many arguments and speeches. At last, in 1789, the Constitution was adopted and the United Colonies became the United States of America.

The first duty of the new nation was to elect a leader, and George Washington was chosen to be the head of the government as the first President of the United States. At noon on April 30, 1789, Washington and the chief justice of the Nation stepped out on the balcony of Federal Hall in New York City. A great crowd stood in the streets below, but all were quiet while George Washington promised to uphold the laws of the United States and to protect the rights of the people.

He had led his countrymen in war and gained independence for the Nation. Now he was to lead them in peace and help to build the solid foundations of a strong and just government. George Washington was the real "Father of His Country," for without his wise and unselfish guidance, the new Nation never would have existed. When the great leader's work was over, he left the United States well fitted to go steadily forward and to grow into a great and prosperous Nation.

REPORTING ON A TOPIC

Read the entire story of The Revolutionary War — George Washington. Your teacher will then give each pupil one of the following topics. Read again that part of the story which describes your topic, and come to the front of the class and tell all that you can about it.

1. George Washington as a surveyor
2. Washington's first duties as a soldier
3. Washington's life in time of peace
4. Commander in chief of the Continental army
5. The Declaration of Independence
6. The capture of Trenton
7. The surrender of Burgoyne

GEORGE WASHINGTON 257

8. Franklin in France
9. The War in the South
10. The story of Yorktown
11. The end of the Revolutionary War
12. From United Colonies to United States

Find on the map in your geography:
The present state of Virginia
The place where the English hoped to divide the colonies
Trenton and Princeton, New Jersey
Yorktown, Virginia
Washington, D. C.

INDEX

Albany, 156, 245
Algonquins, 174, 175–176
Adams, John, 238, 252
Adams, Samuel, 221, 224, 225, 226, 227
Africa, 4
America: discovered, 13, 14; named, 21
Animals found in New World, 35–36
Appalachian Mountains, 197
Arizona, 66
Arkansas, 63
Arkansas River, 183
Armada, Spanish, 83–86
Army, American, 229
Articles of Confederation, 254
Autobiography, of Franklin, 211–212
Aztecs, 34–35, 46, 50–51, 52
Aztec temple, 51, 55

Bahama Islands, 40
Bimini, 39
Boston, 127, 216, 229, 236–237
Boston Massacre, 223
Boston Tea Party, 224–225
Bowery, origin of name, 167
Braddock, General, 200
Brazil, 79
Brewster, Elder, 116
British: at Long Island, 240; at Philadelphia, 241–242; campaign in South, 248; difficulties in war, 249; invade Canada, 244; occupy Philadelphia, 247; surrender at Yorktown, 249–250
Buffalo, 67
Bunker Hill, Battle, 237
Burgoyne, General, 244, 245, 247
Byrd, Commander Richard, 34

Cabot, John: sails west to find China, 88; lands in Newfoundland, 88
California, claimed by Drake for England, 82
Canada: British sail to, 237; French in, 170–179; invasion of, 244
Canary Islands, 10, 11
Cape Charles, 99
Cape Cod, 116
Cape Henry, 99
Catskill Landing, 155
Central America, 71
Carver, John, 116
Champlain, Samuel de: boyhood, 170; friendship for Indians, 177–178; settles Quebec, 173–174; voyages to Spanish America, 171–172
Chesapeake Bay, 107
China, 2, 5
Church of England, 112, 113
Cibola, story of, 64, 66

"Circular Letter," 222
Clinton, General, 250
Cocoa, used by Indians, 35
Colonies: government, 209; population, 209; receive aid from France, 247; rights and duties disputed, 213–225; rebel against taxes, 214–215; seek independence, 238
Columbus, Bartolomeo, 1, 2
Columbus, Christopher: boyhood, 1–3; death, 16, 18; discovers America, 13, 14; first voyage, 12–13; later voyages, 16; made admiral, 8; plans for search for route to East, 5, 6; return to Spain, 15; second homecoming, 16; second voyage, 15; seeks aid from Portugal, 5; seeks aid from Spain, 7; sets sail, 9; studies navigation, 4
Columbus, Diego, 6, 8
Commerce. See *Trade*
Committee of Correspondence, 224, 226
Committee to draft Declaration, 238
Compass, 103, 104
Compostella, 66
Concord, 226, 227, 228
Confederation, Articles of, 254
Congress: Articles of Confederation, 254; First Continental, 225, 235; Franklin's plan, 210; Second Continental, 229, 236; sends Franklin to France, 246
Constitution, adopted, 255
Continental army, 236–237
Continental Congress: adopts Declaration, 238; First, 225, 235; Second, 229, 236
Coronado, Francisco, 64, 66
Corn, in West Indies, 35
Cornwallis: at Yorktown, 250; defeated at Princeton, 244
Cortés, Hernando: attacked by Aztecs, 53–55; boyhood, 45; expedition to West Indies, 45–46; in Mexico City, 57–59
Coureurs de bois, 178
Croatan, 95, 96
Cuba, 47

Dare, Virginia, 94, 96
Delaware River, 145, 241
De Soto, Ferdinand, story of, 61–64
Dinwiddie, Governor, 198, 233, 234
Discovery, the, 157, 158
Dorchester Heights, 237
Drake, Sir Francis: adventures along coast, 79–80; boyhood, 73; knighted, 83; plans revenge on Spanish, 75–76; returns to England, 81; secures Spanish treasure, 81; visits Raleigh's colony, 93; voyage around world, 82; voyage to West Indies, 74–75

INDEX

Dutch: aided by England, 83; under Spanish rule, 83
Dutch East India Company, 151, 152, 156
Dutch West India Company, 167
Duxbury, 125

Earth, theory of form, 5, 32
East, Columbus' second search for, 15–18
East, trade routes, 2–6, 15
East Indies, 2, 3, 5, 7, 14, 29, 32, 107
Elizabeth, Queen, 75, 82, 92
England: at war with colonies, 236–251; at war with France, 199; claims land in New World, 197, 198; claims New Netherland, 165, 166; colonizes America, 88–110, 112–126, 143–144; persecutes Puritans, 112–114; seeks Northwest Passage, 150–151; seeks western route, 88–89; taxes colonies, 236–251
"English pirates," 83
Explorations: Central America, 71–72; early Spanish, 36–37; for gold, 45–48, 60–61, 71; in Florida, 36–44; in North America, 15–18; in Southwest, 60–71; South America, 25–28

Fairfax, Lord, 232
Farming, West Indies, 35–36
Ferdinand, King, 7, 8, 14, 15, 41
Florida: colonized by Spain, 43–44; discovery, 40–41; expeditions to, by De Soto, 61–63
First Continental Congress, 225, 235
First English colony, 92
Fort Duquesne, 199, 201–202, 203
Fort Niagara, 203
Fort Pitt, 203
Fort St. Louis, 194, 195, 196
Fountain of Youth, 38, 42–43
Fox River, 183
France: at war with England, 197–199; aids colonies, 246; her part in Revolution, 246, 247, 250, 252; treaty with colonies, 248–249
Franklin, Benjamin: drafts Declaration, 238; in France, 246, 252; in Philadelphia, 211–212; inventions, 213; plans Congress, 210; pleads cause of colonies, 220–221; *Poor Richard's Almanac*, 211–212
Fredericksburg, 231
French: aid colonies, 246; and Indian War, 199–205; claim Ohio River Valley, 198; explore Mississippi, 181–183; in Canada, 170–179; in Revolution, 246, 247, 250, 252
French and Indian War, 199–205
Friends, Society of. See *Quakers*
Frontenac, 182
Fur trading, 177, 178, 185–186, 190

Gates, General, 245
Genoa, birthplace of Columbus, 2
Georgia, 62, 248
Germany: colonizes Pennsylvania, 144–145; supplies Hessian troops, 238
Gilbert, Sir Humphrey, 91
Gold, search for, 45–48, 60–61, 67, 77, 105–106
Golden Hind, 79, 81, 82, 83
Government, of United States, adopted, 255

Grand Canyon, 66, 67
Green Bay, 183
Greene, General, 249–250
Greenland, 150
Griffin, the, 185, 189
Gulf of Mexico, 195, 196

Half Moon, the, 152, 153, 154, 156
Haiti, settled, 15–16
Hancock, John, 226, 227
Henry, Patrick, 218–219, 226
Henry the Seventh, 89
Hessians, 238, 240, 242
Holland, 113–114
Horses, brought to America by Spaniards, 35
House of Burgesses, Virginia, 235
Howe, General, 237, 240, 244, 247
Hudson Bay, 158
Hudson, Henry: adventures on *Half Moon*, 154–155; cruises along coast, 153; explores Husdon River, 153, 154; hardships on *Discovery*, 158–159; in Hudson Bay, 157–159; last voyage, 157–159; seeks Northwest Passage, 150
Hudson, John, 150
Hudson River, 156, 239, 245
Hurons, 174, 177

Illinois Indians, 187–190
Incas, 60–61
Independence, Declaration of, 238
Independence Hall, 255
India, trade with, 2, 5, 88, 157
Indians: Algonquin, 174–176; along the Mississippi, 183; and Magellan, 26; and Smith's colony, 102–104; attack mission, 69–71; first named such by Columbus, 14; friendship for French, 174; friendship for Hudson, 155; Illinois, 187–190; in Florida, 42–43, 62–63; in Mexico, 46–47, 55–56; in French and Indian War, 199; in Pennsylvania, 144; in Raleigh's colony, 93, 94, Iroquois, 174, 175–176, 184, 187–188, 190, 199; Narragansetts, 131–134; on Manhattan, 154; Pequots, 133, 134
Indian corn, 123, 124
Indian Ocean, 31
Invincible Armada, story, 84–86
Ireland, Penn is sent to, 140
Iroquois, 174, 175–176, 184, 187–188, 190, 199
Italy, trade, 2
Isabella, Queen, 7, 8, 14, 15, 16

James River, 99
Jamestown, 98–102, 105–106, 107–109
Jay, John, 252
Jefferson, Thomas, 238
Joliet, 183

Kansas, 67
King Charles, 142
King George III, 213, 215, 224, 238
King James, 101, 113, 115, 157
King Louis of France, 194

Labrador, 157
Ladrone Islands, 30
Lady Rebecca, 110

INDEX

Lafayette, Marquis de, 246, 250, 252
Lake Champlain, 175, 239
La Chine, 172
Lake Huron, 177
Lake Michigan, 183
Lake Ontario, 203
Lake Peoria, 187
La Rabida, Convent of, 6
La Salle, Robert: commands Fort Frontenac, 184; death, 195; encounters Indians, 187–188; explorations along Mississippi, 184, 185–186, 189, 190, 191–192; returns to France, 194
Lee, Richard Henry, 238
Legend of Fountain of Youth, 38
Lexington, 226, 227
Leyden, 113
Livingston, Philip, 238
London Company, 105, 111
Long Island, Battle, 239–240
Lost Colony, 96
Louisburg, 202
Louisiana, 194

Magellan, Ferdinand: at Spice Islands, 31; death, 31; discovers Ladrone Islands, 30; discovers strait, 27–28; in Philippines, 31; in South America, 26; seeks trade route to Indies, 22, 23; voyage, 24
Manhattan, 153
Manhattan Island, bought from Indians, 161
Marcos, Friar, story, 65–66
Marina, 48, 56
Marion, Francis, 248
Marquette, 183
Massachusetts: adopts resolutions, 219; Committee of Correspondence, 224, 226
Massachusetts Bay colony, 127, 129, 130, 133
Massasoit, 122, 130
Mayflower, the, 115, 119, 120
Mayflower Compact, 116
Mexico, conquered by Cortés, 46–50
Mexico City, story, 49–59
Minuit, Peter, 131
Minutemen, 226, 228
Missionaries, story of, in Southwest, 66–67
Mississippi, the: discovery, 63; explorations, 182–184, 185–186, 189, 190–192
Montcalm, General, 203, 204
Monterey, 69
Montezuma, story of, 50–55
Montreal, 177
Moors, at war with Spain, 7
Mount Vernon, 235, 254
Mount Royal, 177
Muscovy Company, 150, 151

Narragansetts, 131–134
Navigation Acts, 214–215
Negroes, as slaves, 36
New Amsterdam, 162, 165
New England: government, 209; origin of name, 110
Newfoundland, 88, 91
New France, 171, 172, 197
New Hampshire, militia, 245
New Jersey, 241

New Mexico, 68
New Netherland, 161, 162, 166
New Orleans, 196
Newport, Captain, 105
New World: animals in, 36; Columbus' description, 34–35; crops, 35
New York: celebration in, 253–254; naming, 167; retreat from, 240–241
Nicolls, Colonel Richard, 166, 167
Niña, 8, 15
North Carolina, Sons of Liberty in, 220
Northwest Passage, search for, 150, 152, 158
Norway, 152
Nova Zembla, 151, 152

Ohio River, 184, 234
Ohio River Valley, story, 198–199
Old North Church, 227
Old South Church, 224
Oxford University, 137, 139, 140

Pacific Ocean, named by Magellan, 29, 82
Palos, 6, 8, 10
Panama Trail, 77
Paris, treaty of peace at, 252
Patagonia, 27
Peace of Paris, 252
Penobscot Bay, 153
Penn, Admiral, 137, 139, 141, 142
Penn, Sir William: boyhood, 137–138; founds Pennsylvania, 143–147; imprisoned, 140; joins Quakers, 140; religious beliefs, 138–140; sails to America, 144; sent to France, 139–140; sent to Ireland, 140; treaty with Indians, 146
Pennsylvania: how named, 143; colonial life in, 145–146
"Pennsylvania Dutch," 145
Pennsylvania Gazette, 211
Pequot Indians, 133–135
Perez, Friar Juan, 6, 7
Philadelphia: army at, 240–242; captured by British, 244–247; First Continental Congress, 225; founding, 147–148
Philip, king of Spain, 74, 77, 82, 83
Philippine Islands, 31, 82
Pilgrims, 113, 115–116, 119–120, 123
Pinta, 8, 10, 15
Pinzon, 9
Pitt, William, 202, 214, 222
Pittsburgh, 203
Pizarro, 60–61
Plains of Abraham, Battle, 205
Plymouth, 85, 115, 119–120
Pocohontas, 104, 109
Polo, Marco, 4
Ponce de Leon, Juan: boyhood, 36–37; death, 43; explores Florida, 40–41; governor of Haiti, 37; return to Spain, 43; seeks Fountain of Youth, 38–40
Poor Richard's Almanac, 211–212
Portugal: refuses aid to Columbus, 5–6; refuses aid to Magellan, 23; seeks trade route, 3, 4; trade with Indies, 16
Potatoes, in West Indies, 35
Potomac River, 107
Powhatan, 104
Prince Henry, 3
Princeton, British defeat at, 244

INDEX

Providence, founding of, 131–133
Puerto Rico, 40, 43
Puritans, 112, 128

Quakers, 138–139, 140, 142
Quebec: battle, 203–205; settling, 173–174
Queen Elizabeth, 74, 75, 77, 82, 83

Raleigh, Sir Walter: boyhood, 90; second colony, 94–95; settles Virginia, 91–94
Revere, Paul, 227
Revolutionary War: campaign in North, 239–246; campaign in South, 248–252; causes, 213–217, 218–220; first battles, 227–229, 237–239; France in, 246–248; results, 252, 253; treaty, 252, 253; Washington commander in, 236–237
Rhode Island, 132
Roanoke, 92, 99
Rolfe, John, 110

Sailors, Columbus', 12–13
Salem, 127
Samoset, 121, 122
San Antonio, 68
San Diego, mission, 69
Santa Fe, 68
Santa Maria, 8, 10, 15
San Francisco, Bay of, 82
Saratoga, Battle, 245
Scotch-Irish, in Penn's colony, 144
"Sea dogs," 74
"Sea of Darkness," 3, 9
Second Continental Congress, 229, 236
Separatists, 113
Serra, Father Junipero, 69, 71
Seven Cities, search for, 66
Sherman, Roger, 238
Slaves, imported from Africa, 36
Smith, Captain John: adventures with Indians, 102–104; answer to London Company, 105–106; joins expedition to Jamestown, 99–100; later voyages, 110; returns to England, 109; rules colony, 101, 107–109; saved by Pocohontas, 104
Smuggling, 215, 216
Sons of Liberty, 220, 226
South, campaign in, 248
South America, 25–28, 60–61
South Carolina, 62, 248
Southwest, missionaries in, 65–66
Spain: aids Magellan, 24; claims Florida, 41–42; Columbus claims land in name of, 14; conquers Moors, 7; conquers Mexico, 45–58; explores for gold, 61; honors Columbus, 15; loses sea control, 86; trouble with England, 83
Spaniards: capture La Salle's ship, 195; clash with Drake, 74–78; ill treat Indians, 62–63; in Central and South America, 60–61, 71–72; in Florida, 35–44, 61–62; in Mexico City, 50–59; in the Southwest, 60–72; search for seven cities, 67–68; seek trade routes, 6–8, 15–18; search for gold, 45–52
Spanish Main, 74, 75
Speedwell, 115
Spitzbergen, 150
Squanto, 121, 122

Stamp Act, 216–217, 218, 219, 221
Standish, Captain Miles, 114, 116, 118, 125
Starved Rock, 194
"Starving Time," 109
States' rights, 255
Stephen, Negro slave, 65
St. Augustine, 41
St. Joseph River, 186
St. Lawrence River, 172
Strait of Mackinac, 185
Strait of Magellan, 29
Stuyvesant, Peter: governor, 162–164; later life, 167–168; New Netherland under his rule, 164–165; surrenders colony, 165, 166.
Swallow, 75
Sun God, legend, 49–50

Tampa Bay, 62
Taxation: between states, 255; Navigation Acts, 214–215; Stamp Act, 216–219; "without representation," 221–222; Writs of Assistance, 216, 221
Tea, tax, 223
Texas, 68
Thanksgiving, first, 124
Tobacco, 35, 93, 110
Tonty, Henry, 185, 189, 190, 191, 194, 195
Trade, early, 2, 3, 4
Tories, 226, 239
Toscanelli, 5
Treaty: French and Indian War, 205; Peace of Paris, 252–253
Trenton, attack on, 242–243
Turkey, found in America, 36

Valley Forge, encampment at, 247
Valparaiso, 79
Vancouver, 82
Vermont, militia, 245
Vespucci, Amerigo, 20
Victoria, the, 31
Virginia, settlement of, 91–92, 93–96

Wall Street, 165
Washington, Augustine, 231
Washington, George: at Fort Duquesne, 200; at Yorktown, 250, 252; boyhood, 231; commander in chief, 229–230, 236–237; delegate to Congress, 235; enters New York, 253–254; inauguration, 256; messenger to French, 199; messenger to the Ohio, 234; pleads cause of army, 242; president, 256; surveyor, 232–233
Washington, Lawrence, 231, 233
Welcome, 145
West India Company, 162
West Indies, 14, 35
White, Governor, 94–96
Williams, Roger: befriended by Indians, 134–135; beliefs, 127–129; brought to trial, 129; flees from Salem, 129–130; founds Providence, 131–133
Wolfe, General, 203–205
Wolfe's Cove, 204
Writs of Assistance, 216, 221

Yorktown, surrender, 249–250

Zunis, the, 65, 66

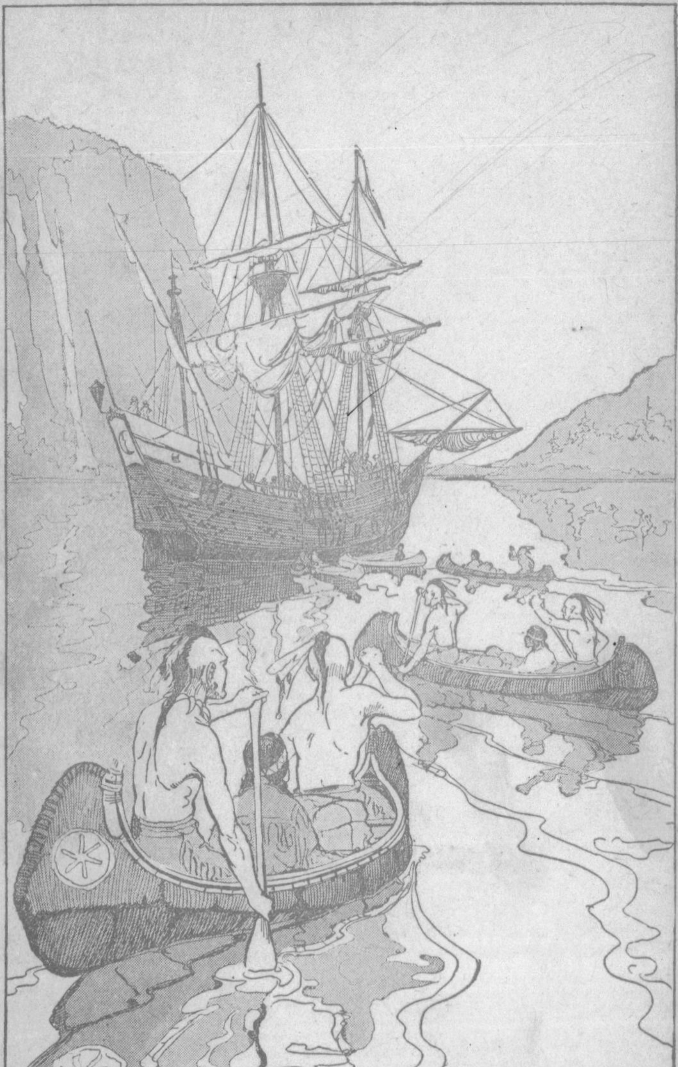